# Young at Heart

# Young at Heart

## A Collection of Drawings and Memories
## from Bill Menzie

Compiled and Introduced by Laurie Menzies

Young at Heart: A Collection of Drawings and Memories
from Bill Menzie

For information about special discounts for bulk purchases,
please contact the publisher.

Embracing Elderhood Press
1745 Hopkins Road
Getzville, NY 14068
716.204.1081

EmbracingElderhoodPress.com
info@EmbracingElderhoodPress.com

Designed and edited by William C. Even
MediaHatchery.com

Manufactured in the United States of America

Library of Congress Control Number: 2016919797

ISBN: 978-0-9906497-2-4 (paperback)

# FOREWORD

I loved being with my Dad. Anytime. Anywhere. We were just happy to be together. I am still learning how to live in this world without him.

He made me a book, *A Father's Legacy*. In it he wrote, "I want people to smile more."

He taught me to "kick the habit" by clicking my heels from side to side as we walked through a parking lot. He always had change in his pocket for a penny bubble gum.

He told me that if I could put salt on a bird's tail, I would be able to catch it. We have home movies of me at the age of two, running through the yard with a salt shaker.

He used to let me do "the wheelbarrow" up the stairs to bed. He always had a candy bar hidden somewhere to bring out as a surprise while we watched TV.

After a night of snow, he would ask, "Did you hear it snow last night? I couldn't sleep, it was so loud!"

When I called from college and asked for a "real" Christmas tree, Mom said they were too expensive. So Dad cut one down from the front of our lawn! (It was beautiful!)

Standing at the back of the Church when my sister married for the second time, Daddy said to her, "I'll keep doing this until you get it right."

I lived with Mom and Dad during law school. I liked to watch the news shows in the morning. Daddy would say, "Why do you want to hear all that bad stuff to start your day? You should decide to be happy instead." Then he would turn off the television and play Jimmy Durante, singing, "You gotta' start off each day with a song, even when things go wrong..."

Two good lines he would say at the end of a party were:

"I've had a nice time .......... but this wasn't it!" or "We've been kicked out of better places than this ...."

After his service in WWII, he drove a trolley and bus for the NFTA. Then he got a job at the post office. He worked hard to support his family, but never put work ahead of us. He didn't derive his sense of self from what he did to make money, but rather by those with whom he shared his life. I can't recall an instance that he didn't have time for me.

Somehow I thought I needed to be the best at everything. Dad wanted me to be happy whatever happened. I always wanted to get an "A" on every exam. When I did, he would say I was a "fart smeller!"

Oh, how he loved to sing. *Everybody Loves Somebody* was his standard (he sang it on stage once, with The Lettermen). He always tried to get everyone to sing *When You're Smiling* with him. We sang his favorite song, *A Dreamer's Holiday*, at my wedding. Daddy was 91 when he finally walked me down the aisle—he sang all night!

His favorite leisure activity was dancing with my Mom. The dance floor would clear and everyone would watch them. They actually won a trip to New York City in a dance contest in 1951. They did a dance called *The Shag*.

He lived longer than he might have because of Mom. I know he tried to stay alive because he didn't want to leave her.

I've never known a greater love than Dad had for Mom. It's the greatest love story I can tell. He loved Mom so much that he gave her another baby after being married for 23 years (me)! They were married 70 years before he died.

Daddy knew Christmas of 2011 would be his last. He asked how much money he had left and said, "Your Mother needs a diamond." They had the best Christmas together, and she got a diamond ring.

He loved pancakes with maple syrup, meatloaf, macaroni & cheese, root beer floats and fried bologna & onions at the ball game.

When I was growing up, my summer nights meant watching baseball with Daddy on the couch. When I was older, we would go to watch the Buffalo Bisons with Mom. The best part of every game was singing *Take Me Out to the Ballgame* and eating Perry's soft ice cream.

Daddy tried to get me to realize that it wasn't anything I did that made him love me; he loved me for just being me. As an example, I remember how useful I felt "holding down" the leaves under the tarp behind the mower … all I had to do was sit there!

He taught me to "direct my feet to the sunny side of the street" and to "let a smile be my umbrella" and that "when you're smiling, the whole world smiles with you." We had a song for everything.

He used to call me on the phone and sing, "I just called to say I love you …"

He was my roller coaster partner. I'll never forget the first time he told me I was big enough to ride the Comet at Crystal Beach! We even rode the Coney Island roller coaster (in Las Vegas) together, when he was 85!

He used to drive down our road with me perched on the back of the convertible so I could wave like Miss America.

He taught me how to sound like the Wizard of Oz by talking through a bedroom window fan.

Daddy asked me a few years ago, "Who wants to live to be 100?" When I didn't know, he said "Probably the guy who is 99!"

He would always say, "I can't wait until tomorrow ..." and, if I forgot and asked why, the same answer always came "... because I get better looking every day!"

At the end of his *Father's Legacy* book, it asked the question, "What word best describes your life?" He wrote: "Happy. We were happy to be together."

He was "alive" every day and content wherever he was, doing whatever was in front of him. He lived with gratitude and humor and tried to make everyone around him happy.

He taught me how to draw and do lettering so I could always make a nice card. We read the comics together every Sunday after church.

He never complained as his physical abilities were taken away or weakened by age. When he couldn't walk, he began to write and draw. At age 94, he would draw a cartoon each day and we would laugh together. Now I share his cartoons with you, so Daddy can give you a smile too.

My Dad truly stayed forever *young at heart*.

— *Laurie Menzies*

4

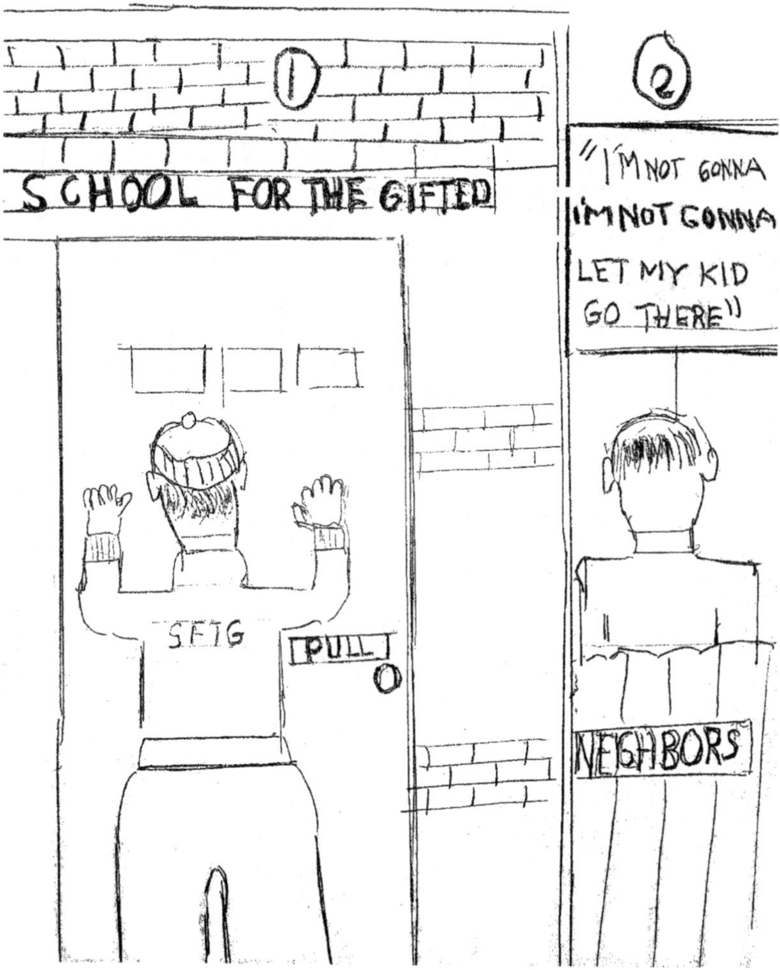
1
SCHOOL FOR THE GIFTED
SFIG
PULL
2
"I'M NOT GONNA
I'M NOT GONNA
LET MY KID
GO THERE"
NEIGHBORS

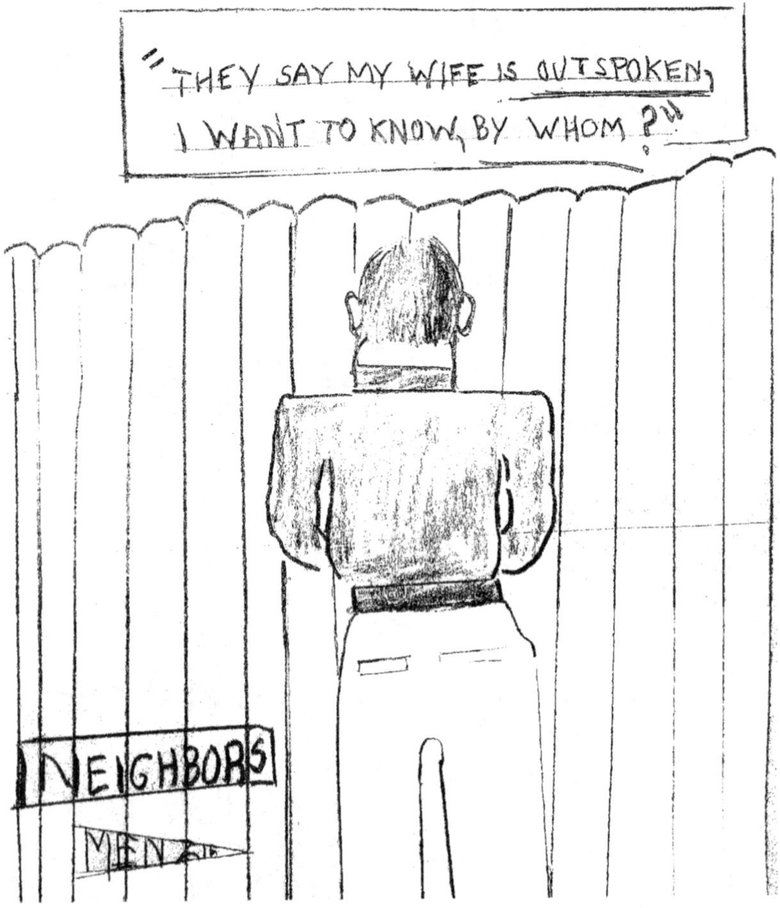
"THEY SAY MY WIFE IS OUTSPOKEN, I WANT TO KNOW, BY WHOM?"
NEIGHBORS

"FRED, YOU EVER WONDER WHAT LIFE'S ALL ABOUT?"
"I HEARD IT'S THE HOKIE POKIE"
NEIGHBORS
MENZIE

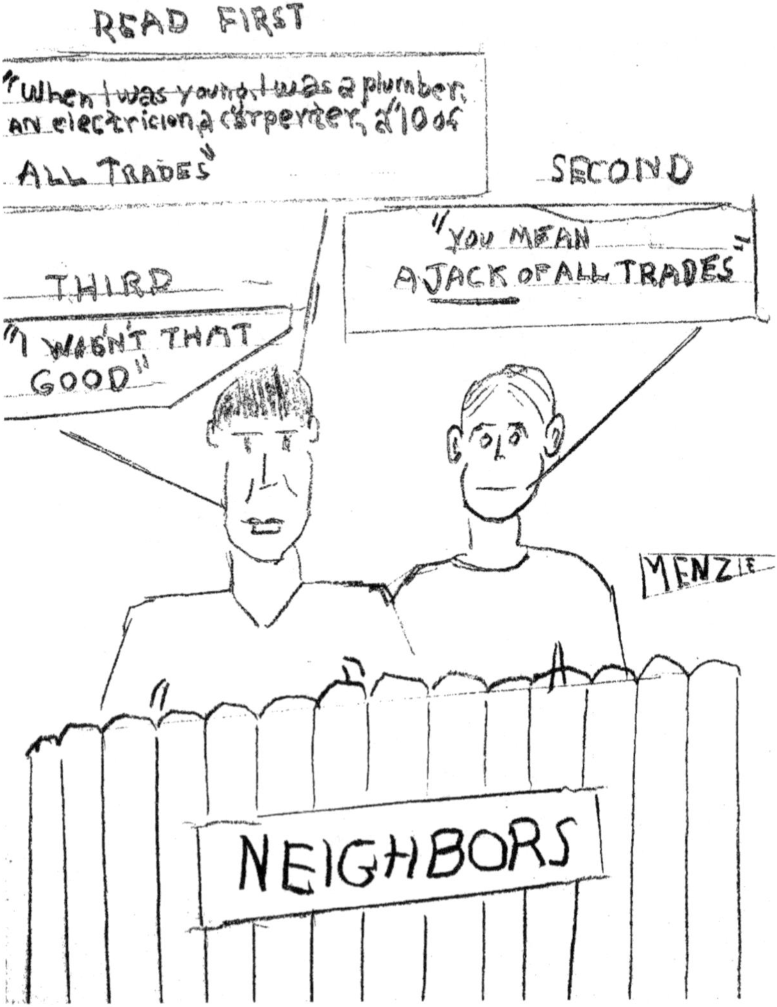
READ FIRST
"When I was young, I was a plumber, an electrician, a carpenter, & 10 of ALL TRADES"
SECOND
"YOU MEAN A JACK OF ALL TRADES"
THIRD
"I WASN'T THAT GOOD"
MENZIE
NEIGHBORS

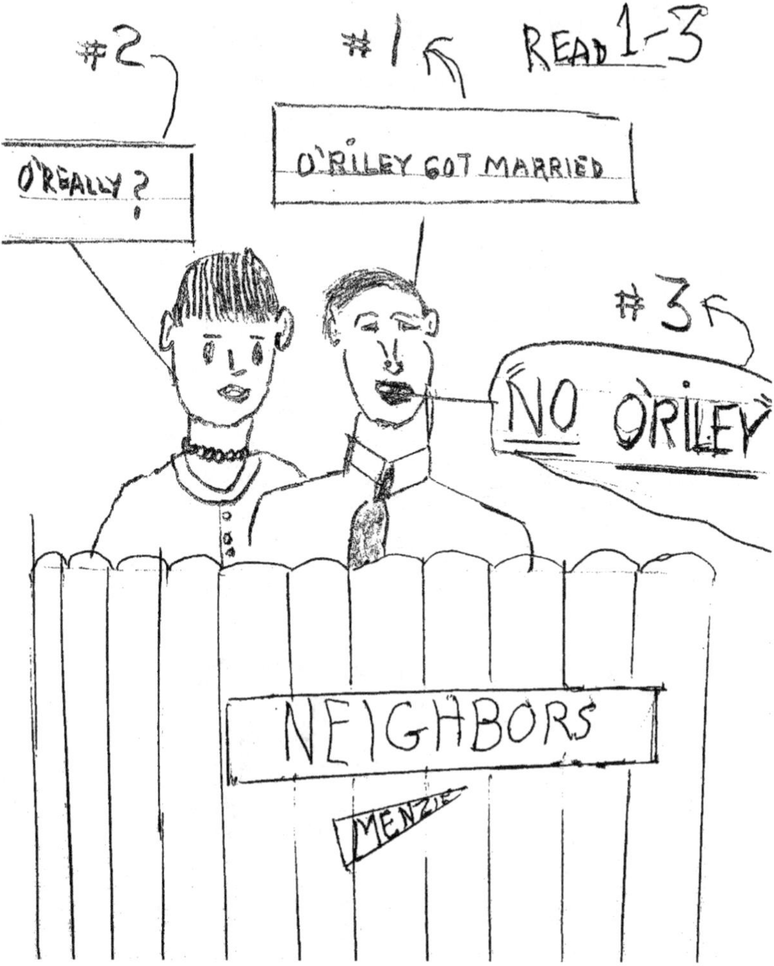
#2
#1
READ 1-3
O'REALLY ?
O'RILEY GOT MARRIED
#3
NO O'RILEY
NEIGHBORS
MENZIE

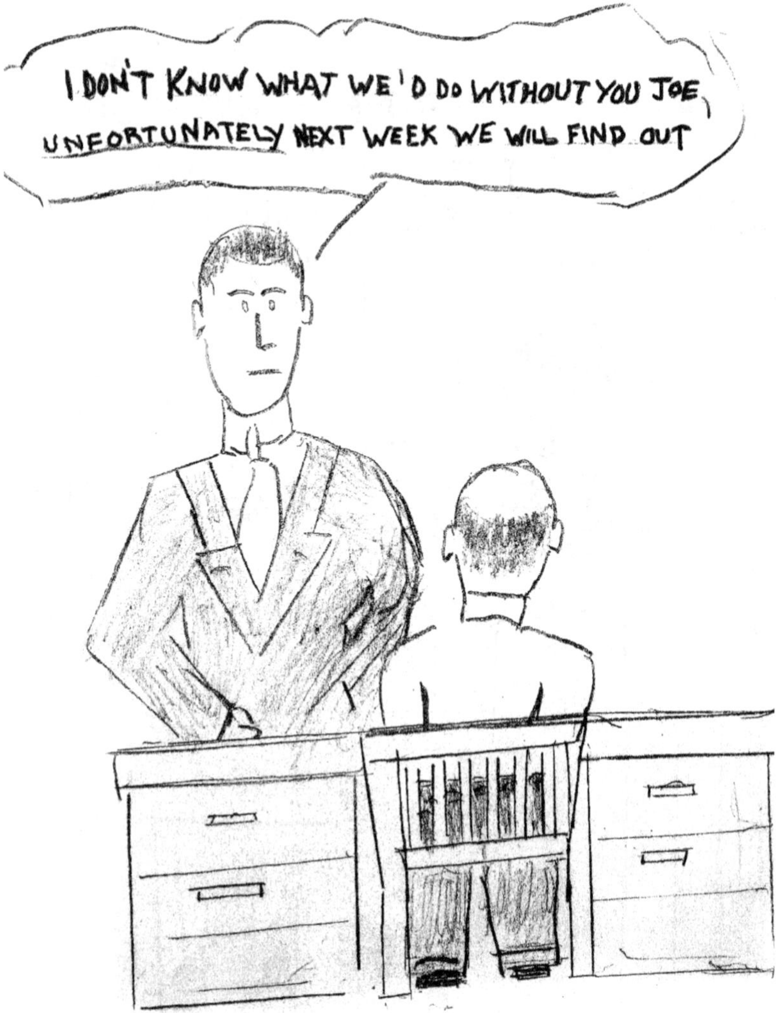
I DON'T KNOW WHAT WE'D DO WITHOUT YOU JOE,
UNFORTUNATELY NEXT WEEK WE WILL FIND OUT

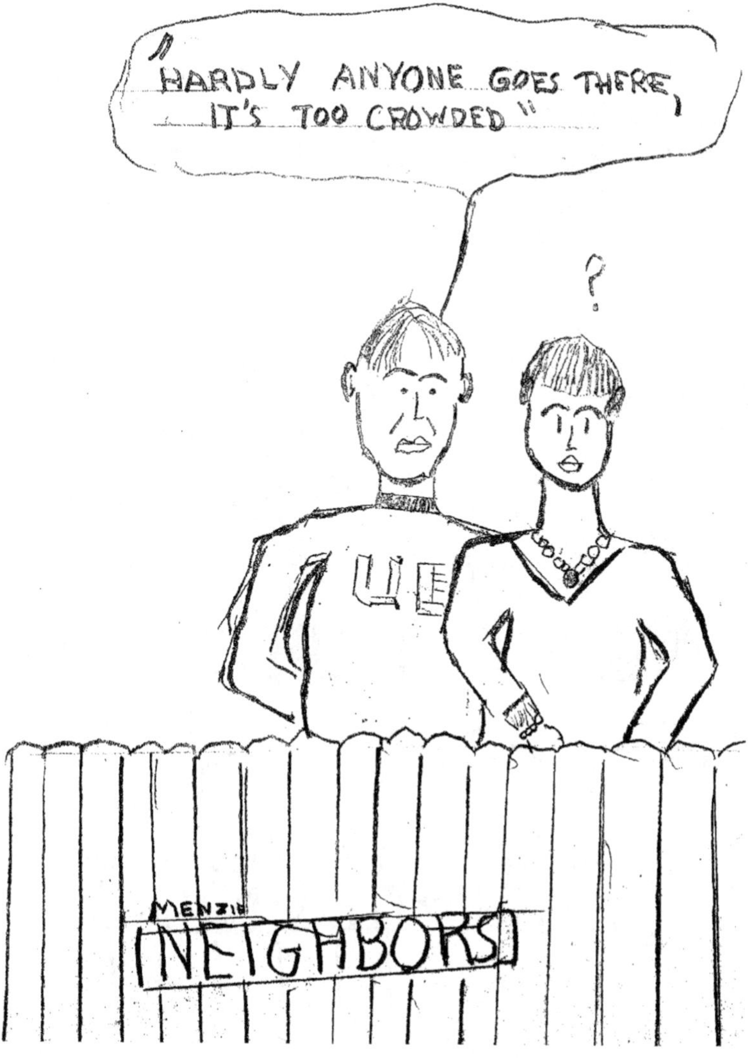
"HARDLY ANYONE GOES THERE, IT'S TOO CROWDED"
?
UE
MENZIE
NEIGHBORS

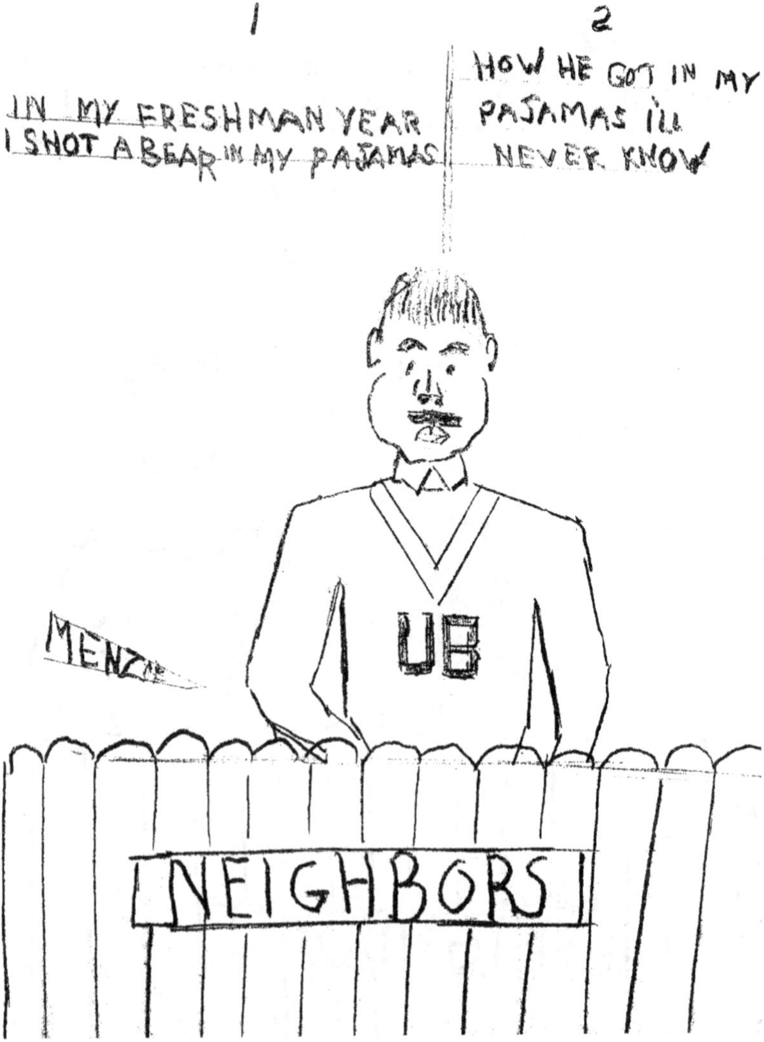
1
2
IN MY FRESHMAN YEAR I SHOT A BEAR IN MY PAJAMAS
HOW HE GOT IN MY PAJAMAS I'LL NEVER KNOW
MENZIE
UB
NEIGHBORS

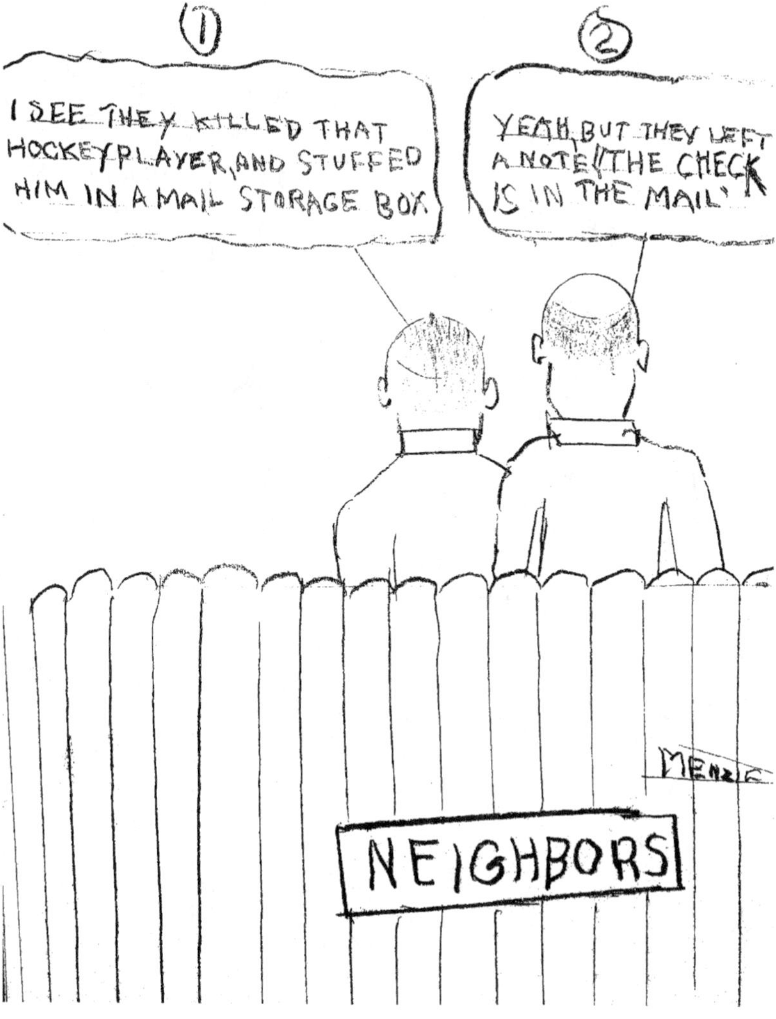
1
I SEE THEY KILLED THAT HOCKEY PLAYER, AND STUFFED HIM IN A MAIL STORAGE BOX
2
YEAH, BUT THEY LEFT A NOTE, "THE CHECK IS IN THE MAIL"
MENZIE
NEIGHBORS

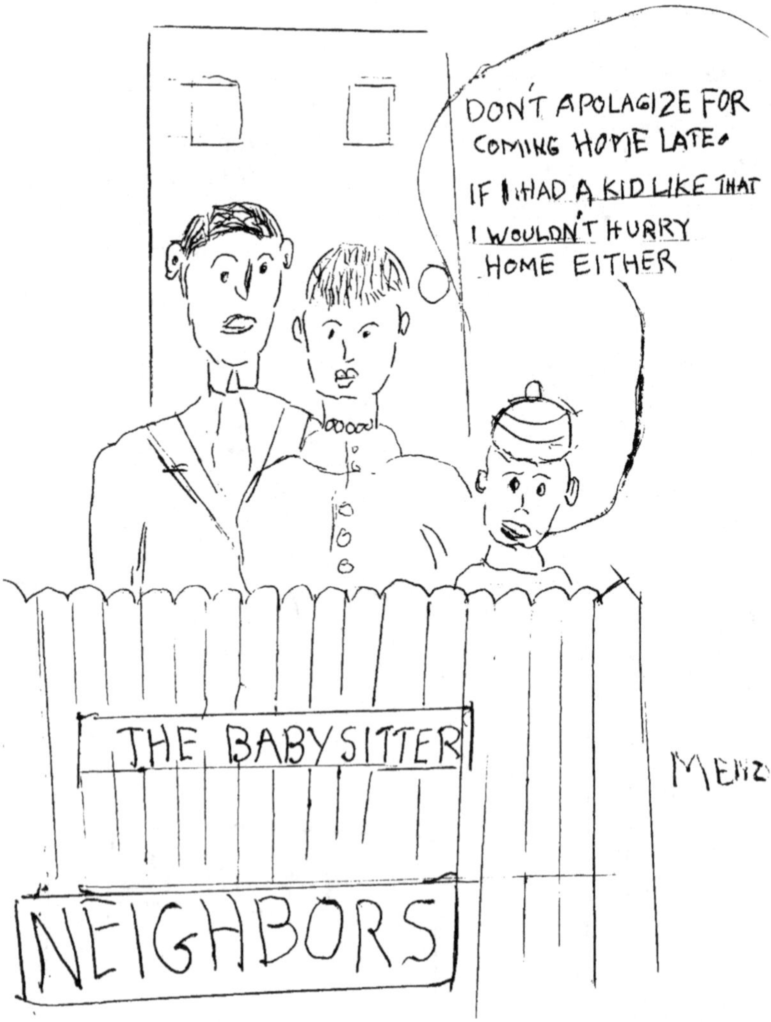
DON'T APOLAGIZE FOR COMING HOME LATE.
IF I HAD A KID LIKE THAT I WOULDN'T HURRY HOME EITHER
THE BABYSITTER
NEIGHBORS

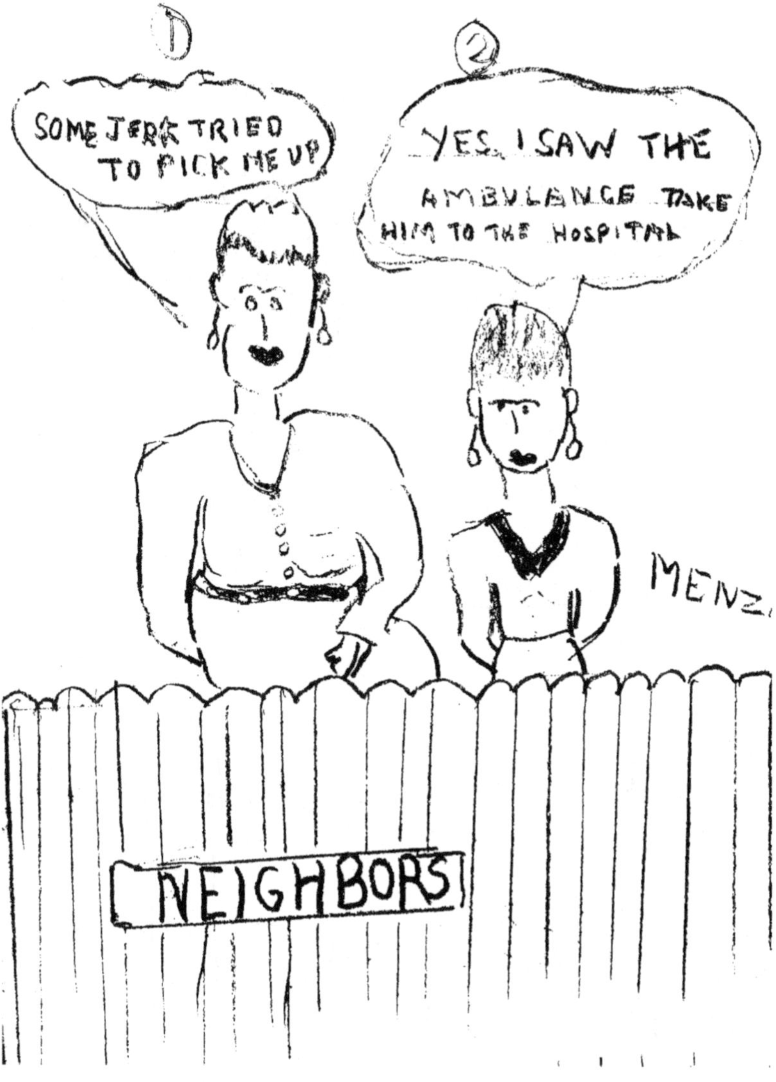
1
SOME JERK TRIED TO PICK ME UP
2
YES, I SAW THE AMBULANCE TAKE HIM TO THE HOSPITAL
MENZ
NEIGHBORS

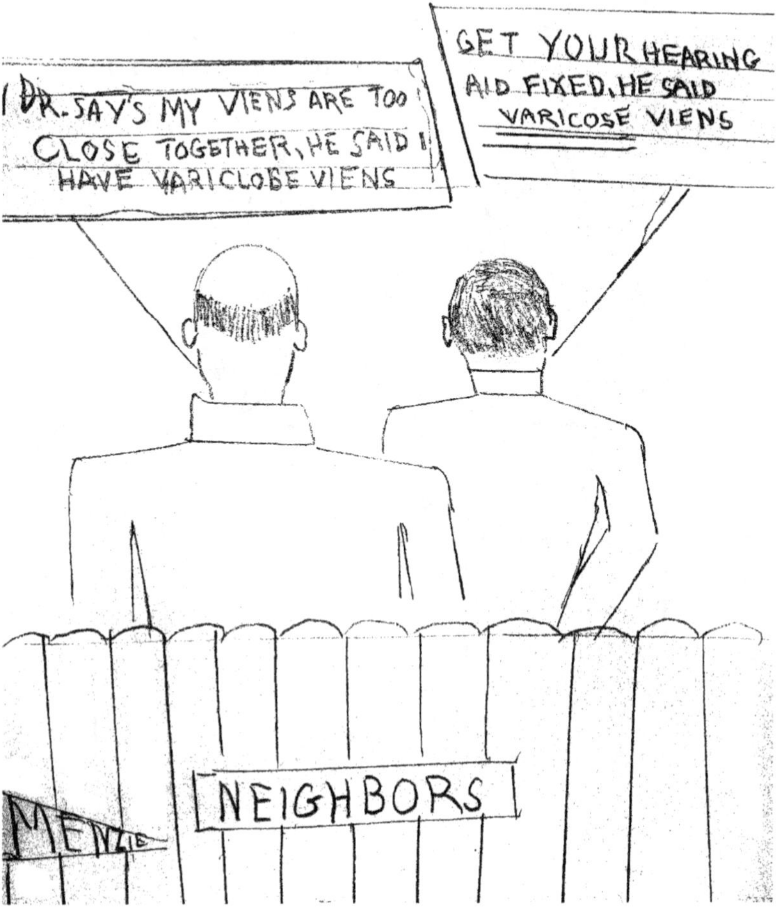
I DR. SAY'S MY VIENS ARE TOO CLOSE TOGETHER, HE SAID I HAVE VARICLOSE VIENS
GET YOUR HEARING AID FIXED. HE SAID VARICOSE VIENS
NEIGHBORS
MENZIE

I Can't wait until tomorrow
I get prettier every day
"A NEIGHBOR"
"Tell your body to WORK OVERTIME!
MENZ
NEIGHBORS

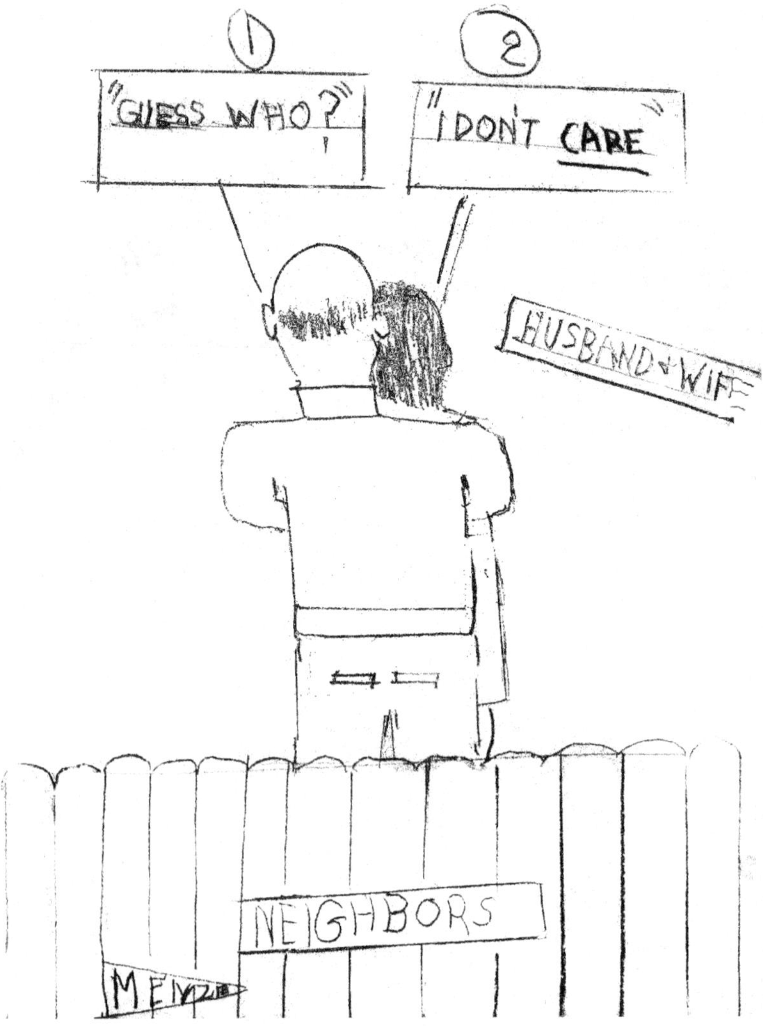
1
"GUESS WHO?"
2
"I DON'T CARE"
HUSBAND + WIFE
NEIGHBORS
MEMZ

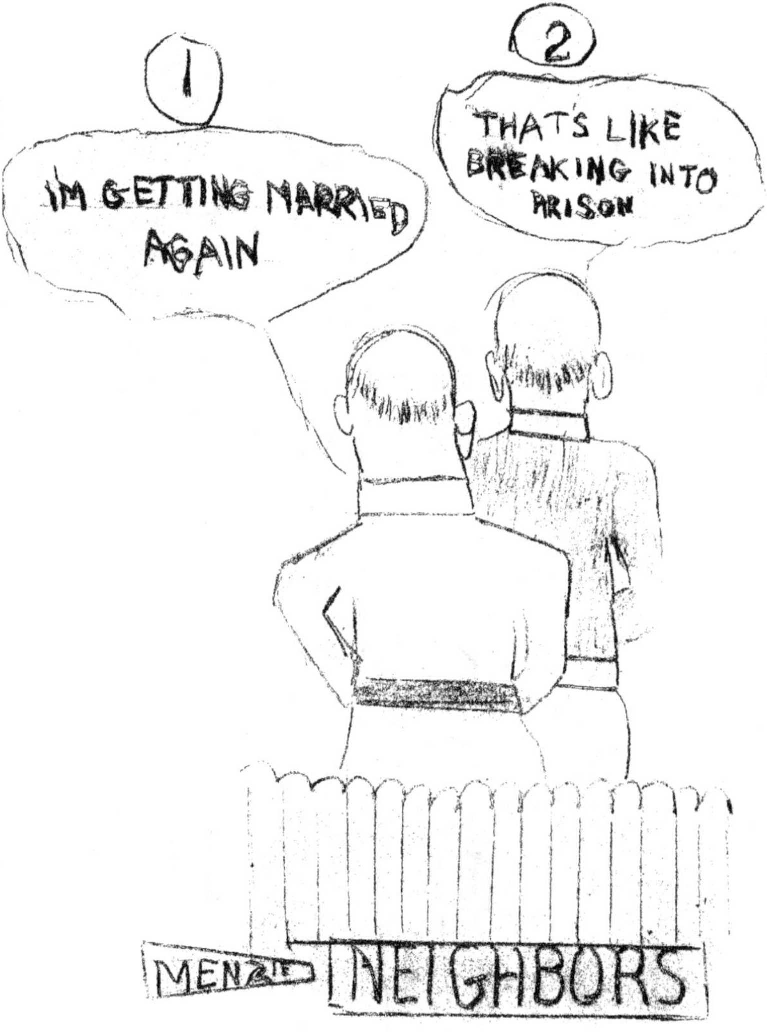
1
IM GETTING MARRIED AGAIN
2
THAT'S LIKE BREAKING INTO PRISON
MENZIE
NEIGHBORS

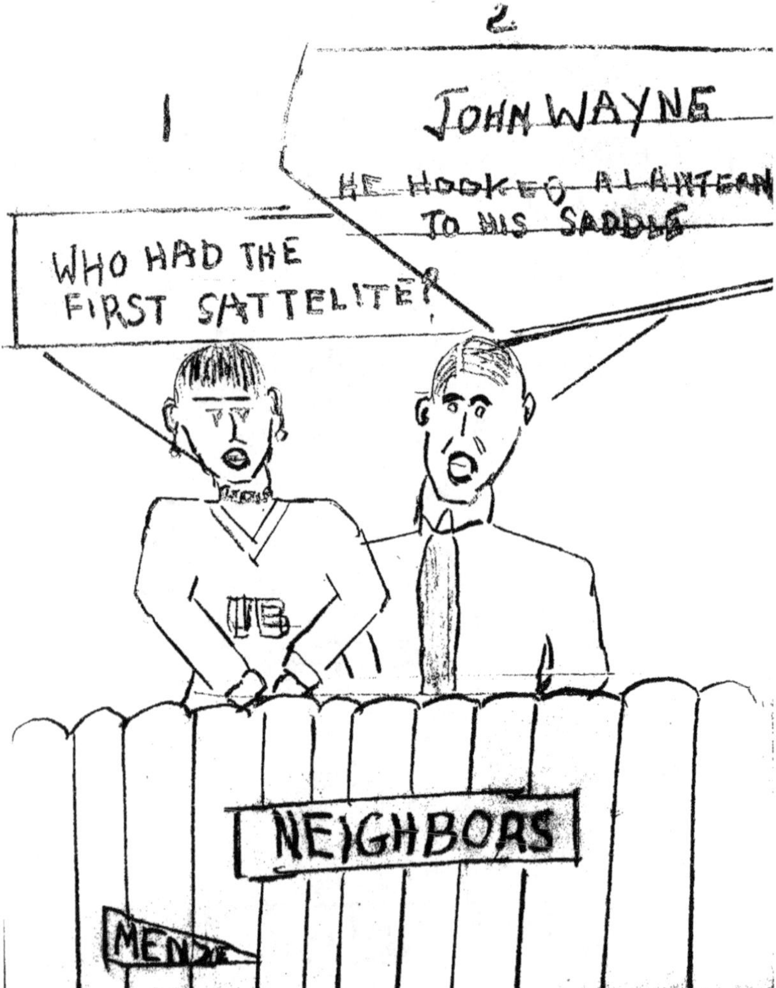
1
WHO HAD THE FIRST SATTELITE?
2
JOHN WAYNE
HE HOOKED A LANTERN TO HIS SADDLE
NEIGHBORS

# SMART CLERK

1
2
I'M IN A HURRY,
2 TENS FOR A FIVE
ALL OUT OF TENS,
I'LL GIVE YOU 4 NEW
ONE'S FOR THAT FIVE
NEIGHBORS

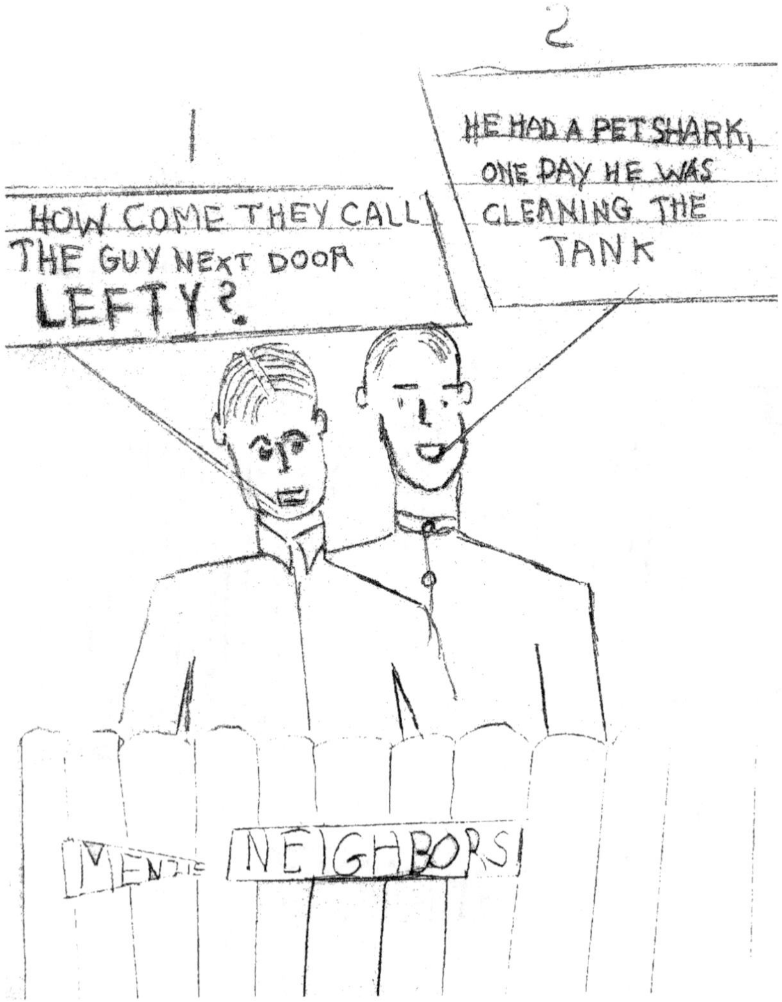
1
HOW COME THEY CALL THE GUY NEXT DOOR LEFTY?
2
HE HAD A PET SHARK, ONE DAY HE WAS CLEANING THE TANK
NEIGHBORS

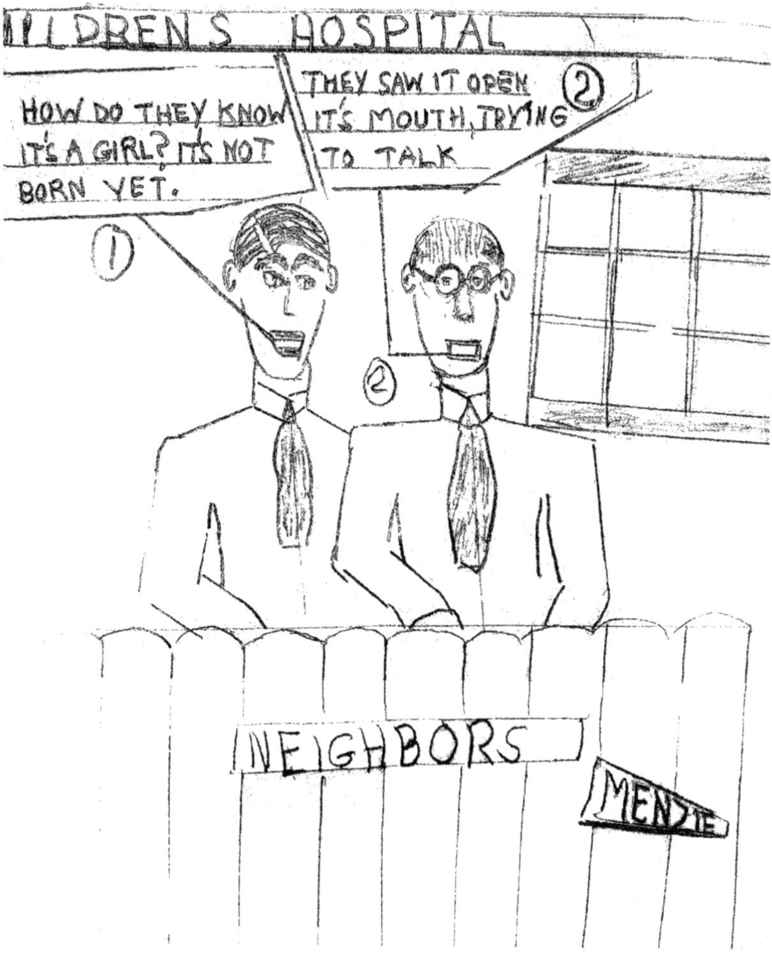

HILDRENS HOSPITAL
HOW DO THEY KNOW IT'S A GIRL? IT'S NOT BORN YET.
THEY SAW IT OPEN IT'S MOUTH, TRYING TO TALK
NEIGHBORS
MENZIE

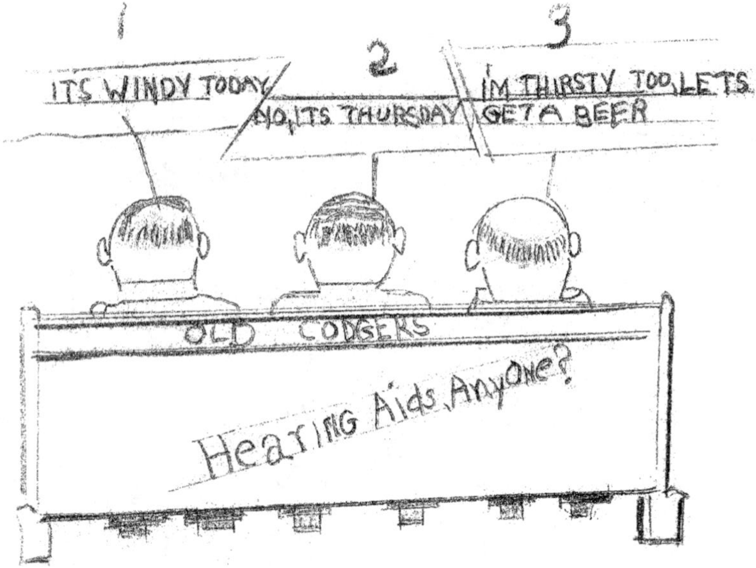
1
ITS WINDY TODAY
2
NO, ITS THURSDAY
3
IM THIRSTY TOO, LETS GET A BEER
OLD CODGERS
Hearing Aids, AnyOne?

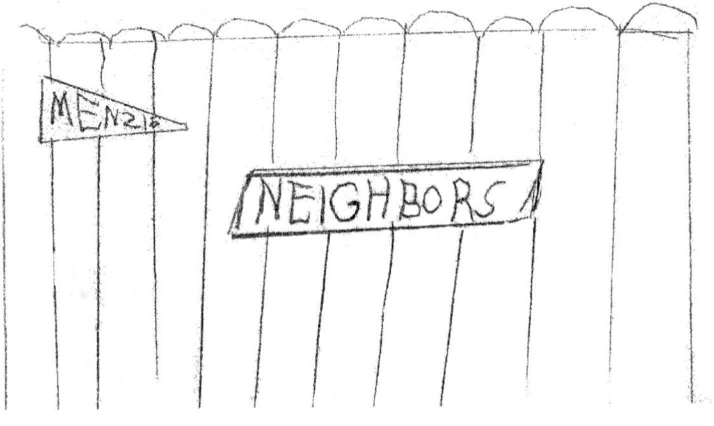
MENZIE
NEIGHBORS

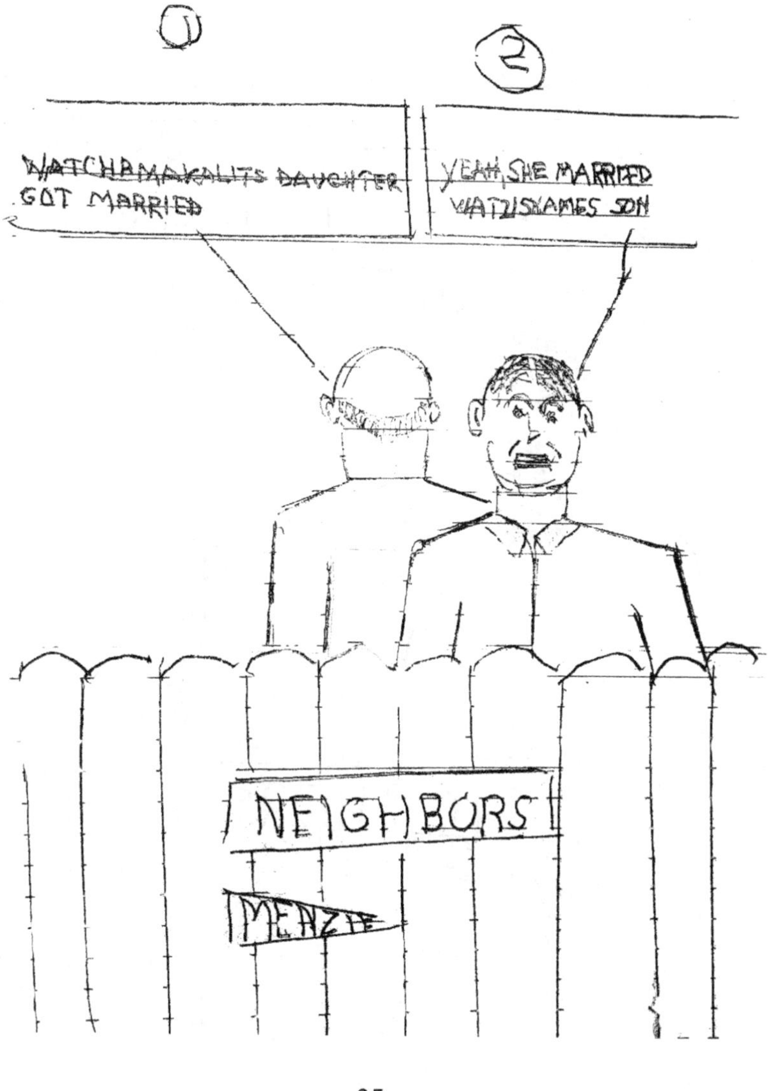
1
2
WATCHAMAKALITS DAUGHTER GOT MARRIED
YEAH, SHE MARRIED WATZISNAMES SON
NEIGHBORS
MENZIE

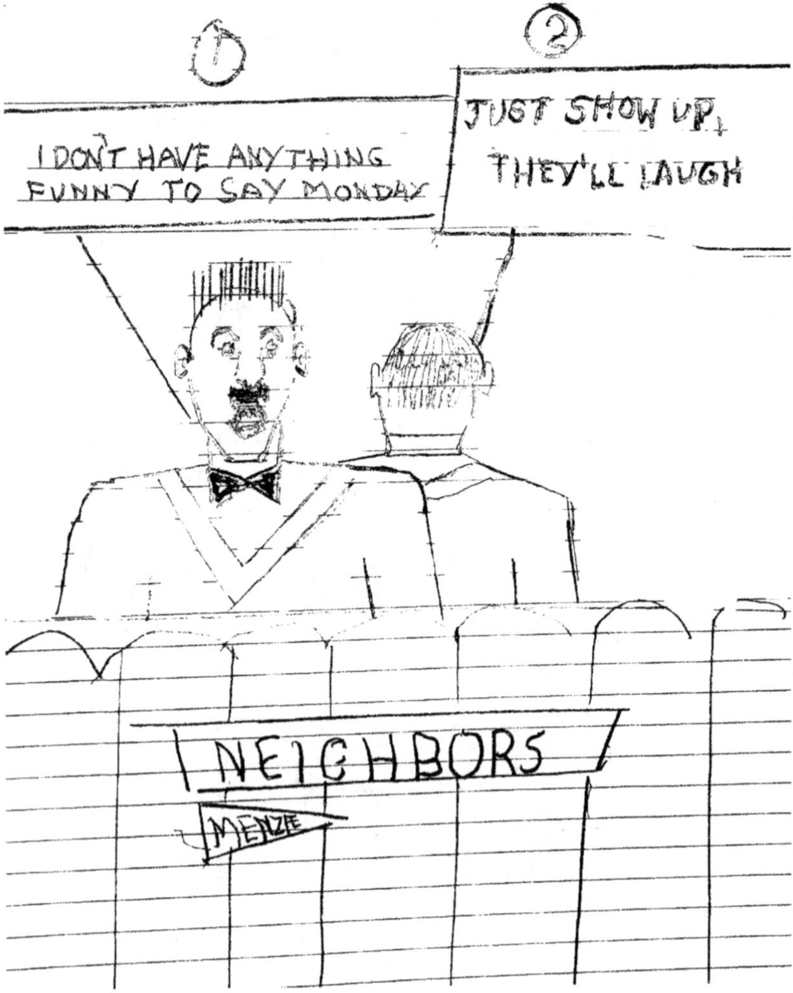
1
I DON'T HAVE ANYTHING FUNNY TO SAY MONDAY
2
JUST SHOW UP, THEY'LL LAUGH
NEIGHBORS
MENZE

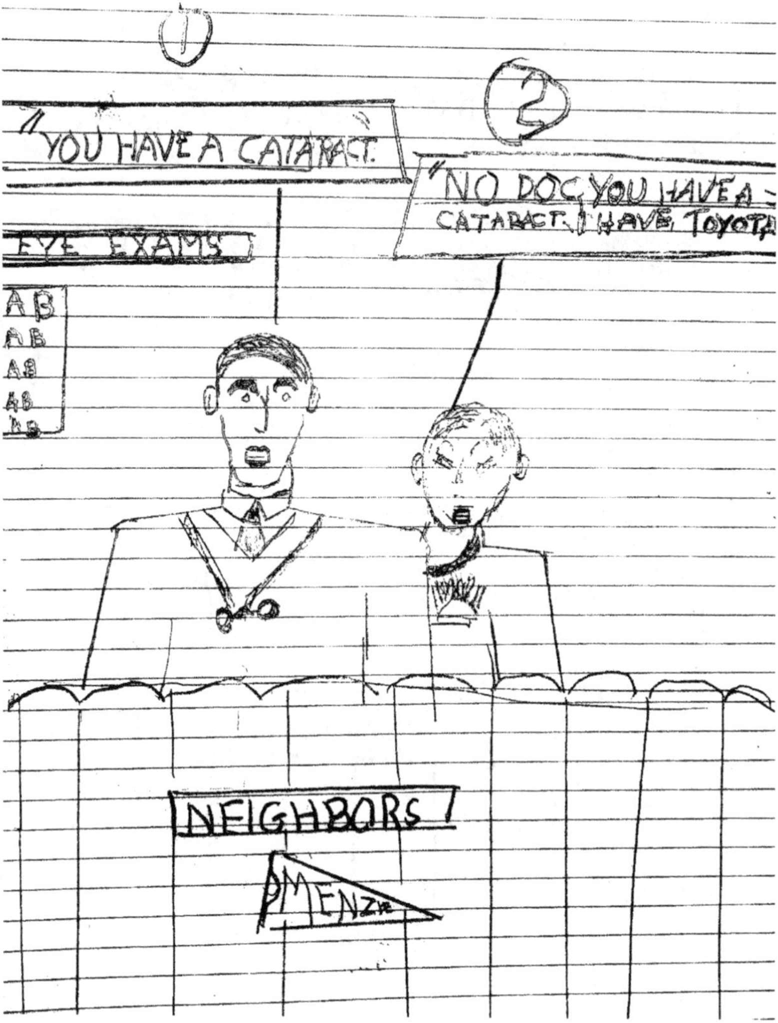
1
"YOU HAVE A CATARACT.
2
"NO DOC, YOU HAVE A CATARACT. I HAVE TOYOTA
EYE EXAMS
NEIGHBORS!

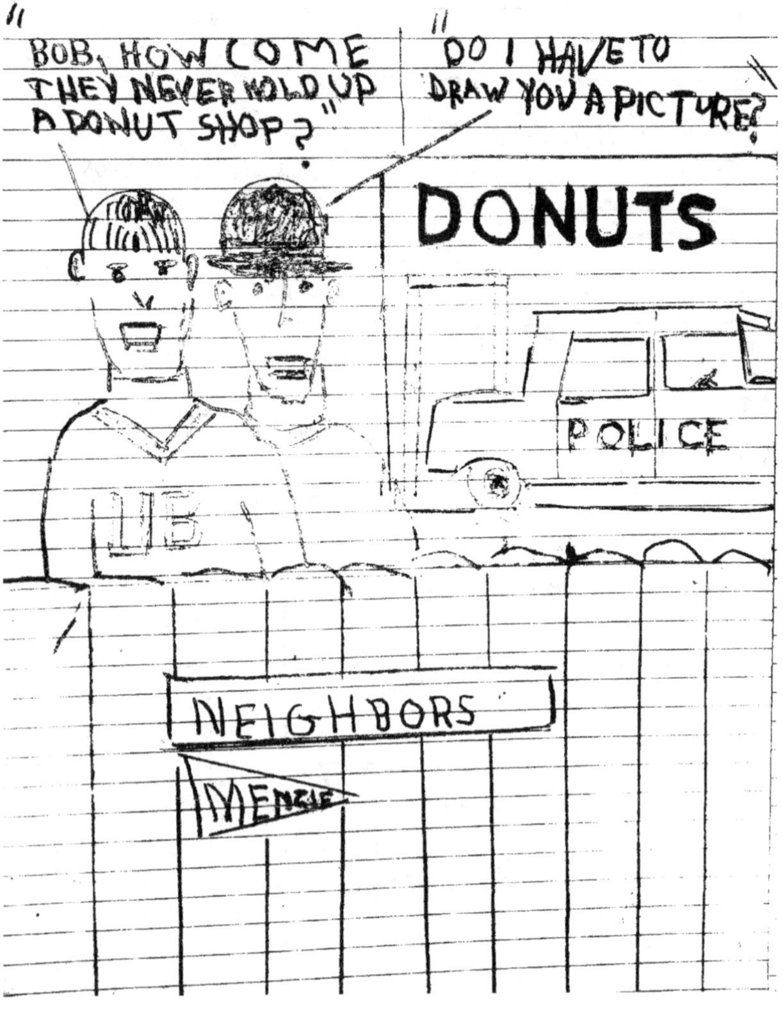
"BOB, HOW COME THEY NEVER HOLD UP A DONUT SHOP?"
"DO I HAVE TO DRAW YOU A PICTURE?"
DONUTS
POLICE
UB
NEIGHBORS

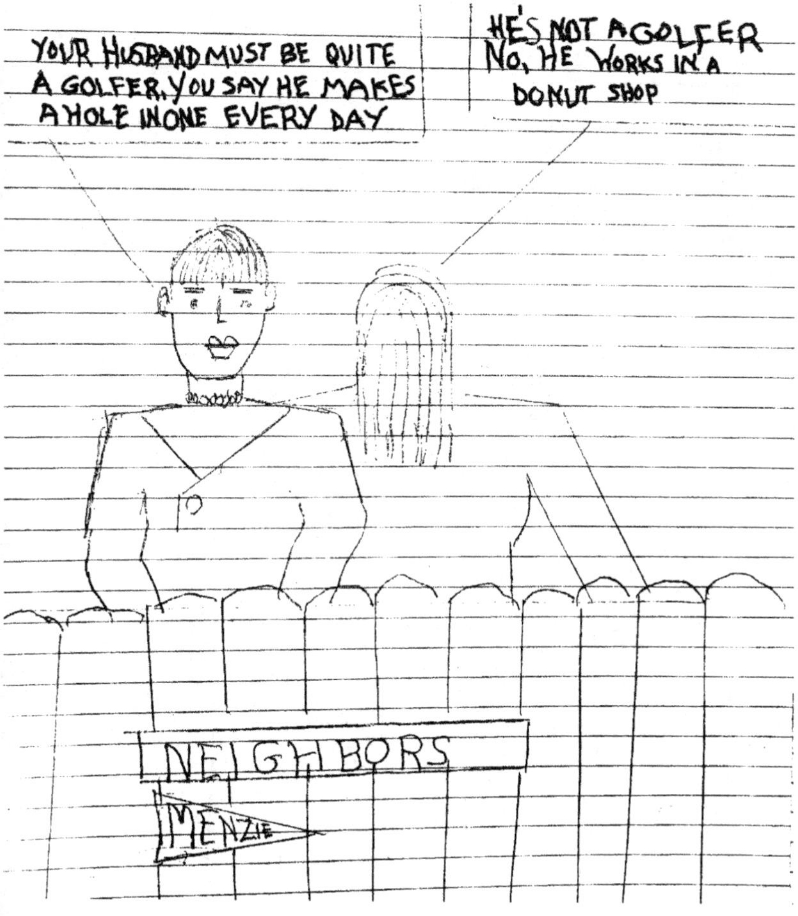
YOUR HUSBAND MUST BE QUITE A GOLFER. YOU SAY HE MAKES A HOLE IN ONE EVERY DAY
HE'S NOT A GOLFER
No, HE WORKS IN A DONUT SHOP
NEIGHBORS
MENZIE

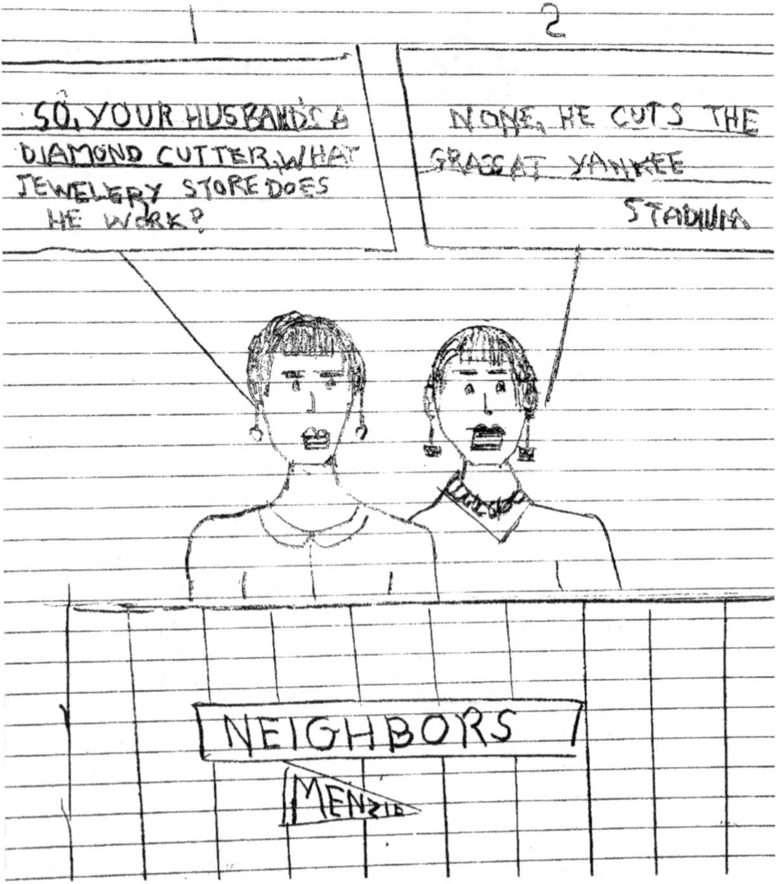
SO, YOUR HUSBAND'S A DIAMOND CUTTER, WHAT JEWELERY STORE DOES HE WORK?
NONE, HE CUTS THE GRASS AT YANKEE STADIUM
NEIGHBORS
MENZIE

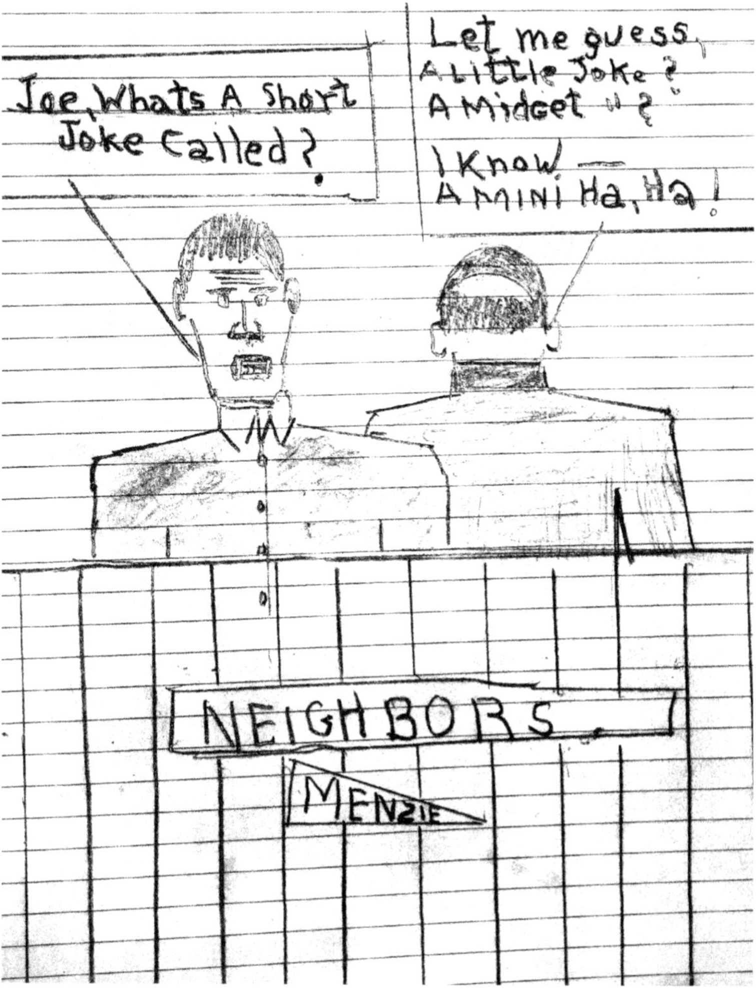
Joe, Whats A Short Joke Called?
Let me guess, A Little Joke? A Midget " ?
I Know — A MINI Ha, Ha!
NEIGHBORS.
MENZIE

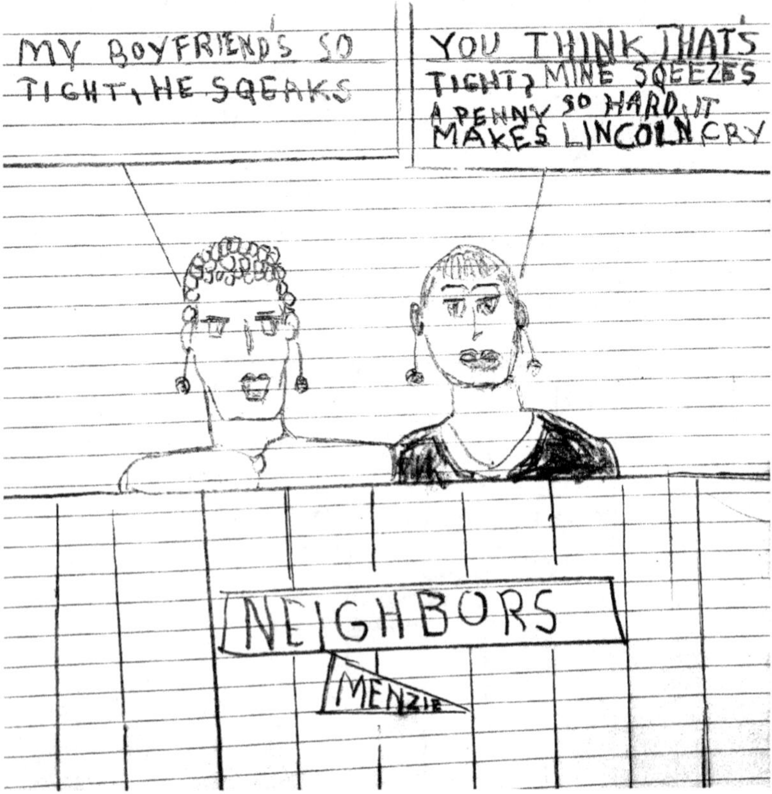
MY BOYFRIEND'S SO TIGHT, HE SQEAKS
YOU THINK THAT'S TIGHT? MINE SQEEZES A PENNY SO HARD, IT MAKES LINCOLN CRY
NEIGHBORS
MENZIE

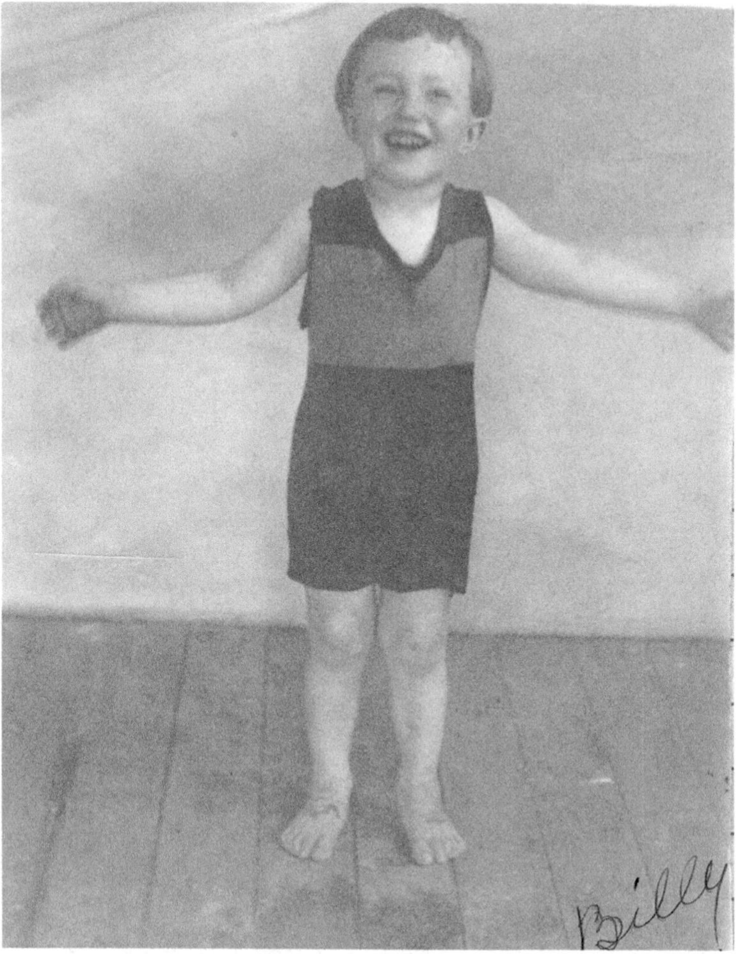
Billy

Daddy, about 3 years old

1942

MR. & MRS.

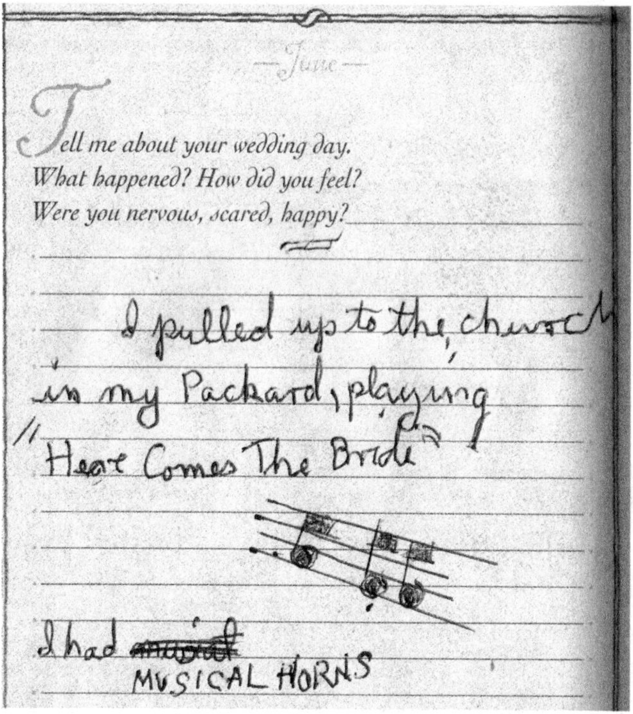

—June—

Tell me about your wedding day.
What happened? How did you feel?
Were you nervous, scared, happy?

I pulled up to the church
in my Packard, playing
"Heare Comes The Bride"

I had ~~music~~
MUSICAL HORNS

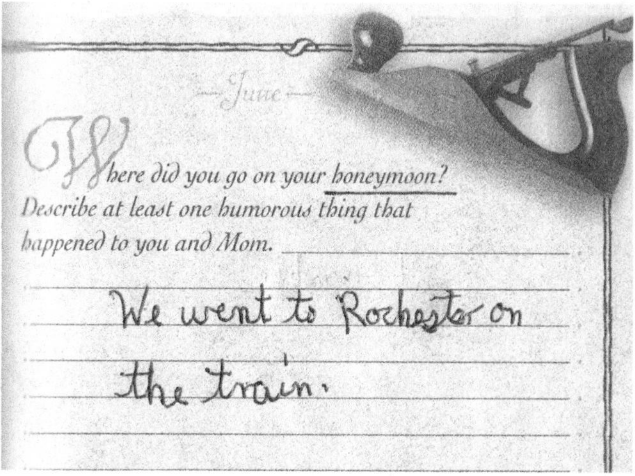

—June—

Where did you go on your honeymoon?
Describe at least one humorous thing that
happened to you and Mom.

We went to Rochester on
the train.

*—April—*

*As a teenager did you rebel or do things your parents wouldn't have approved of? How do you feel about that now?*

No, I didnt.

BILL + DOROTHY WIN A TRIP TO NY CITY !

In 1950 your Mother + I won a dance contest, worth $100.00 Big Money, Them day's

P.S. We took the train.

P.S. 2: We didnt have a Magazine so we didnt go to Baltimore.

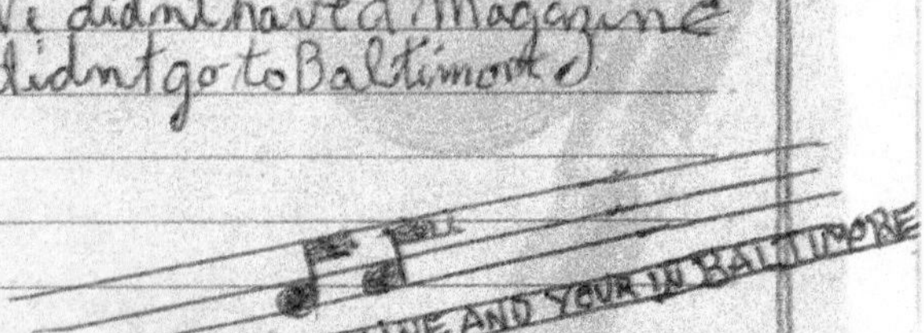
READ AMAGAZINE AND YOUR IN BALTIMORE

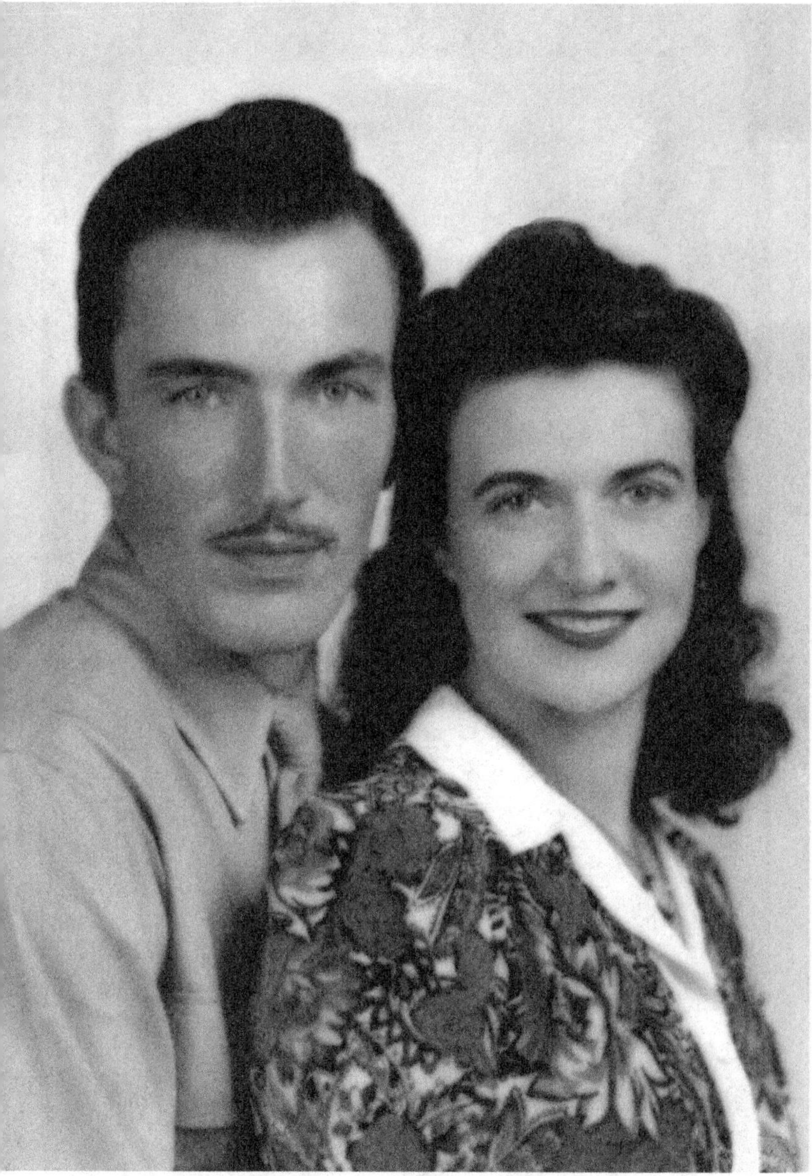

Bill and Dorothy — 1941

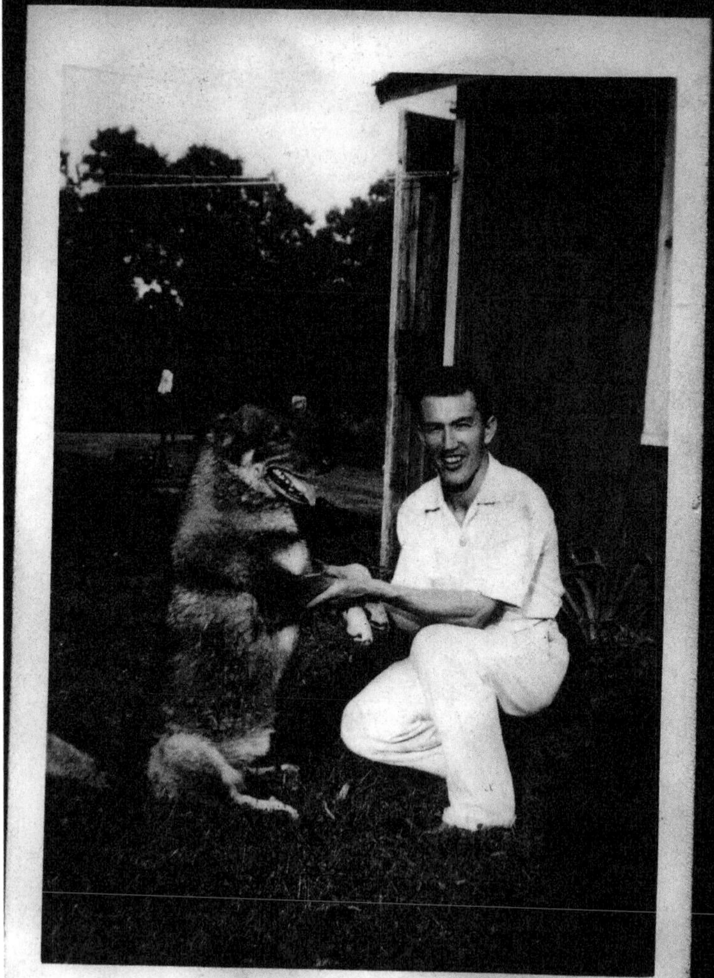

REX AND BILL
JULY '40

*What were your family finances like when you were growing up? How did that affect you?*

Growing up in the Depreshen, very few had much money. It made you appćiate things later on in life.

~ EXAMPEL ~

ON THANKSGIVING

My Father would walk thru the dining room with a picture of a Turkey, while we were eating our P.B. sandwiches.

—March—

*Did you have a television when you were growing up? What was your favorite program? Why?*

No, Television didnt become popular until after World War II.

We listend to stories + music on the radio.

↓

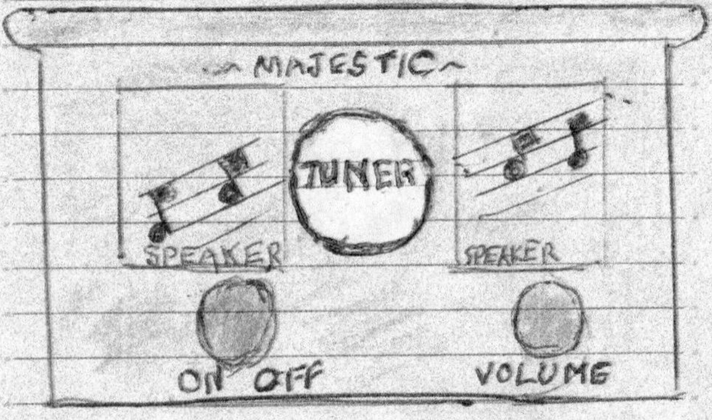
MAJESTIC
TUNER
SPEAKER
SPEAKER
ON OFF
VOLUME

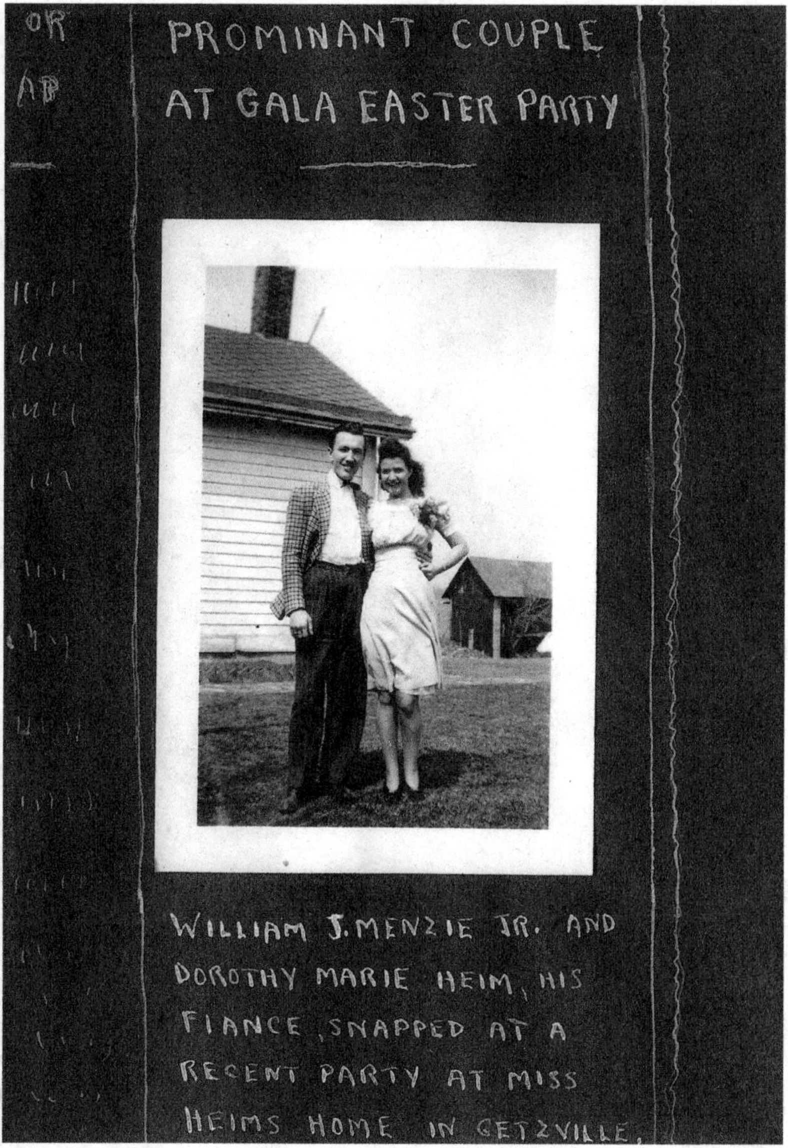
PROMINANT COUPLE
AT GALA EASTER PARTY
WILLIAM J. MENZIE JR. AND
DOROTHY MARIE HEIM, HIS
FIANCE, SNAPPED AT A
RECENT PARTY AT MISS
HEIMS HOME IN GETZVILLE.

The Future Mr. and Mrs. Menzie

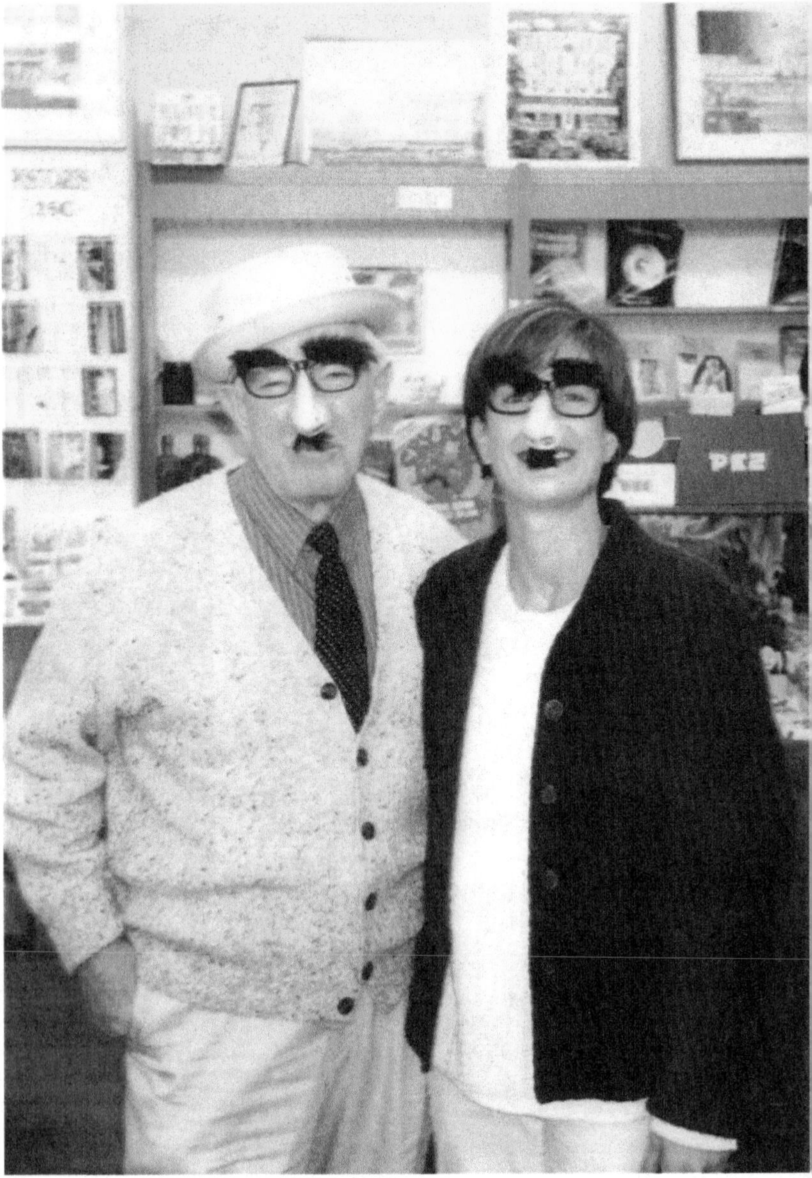
PEZ

Spending the Day at Vidler's in East Aurora

Recall for me ~~from~~ One
of the most important lessons
you have learned in life.

"Never give two tens for
a five."

*What were some crazy fads from your school days? Did you participate in them? Why or why not?*

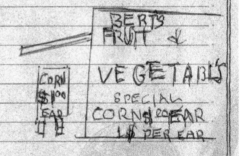

BERTS
FRUIT &
VEGETABLES
SPECIAL
CORN $1.00 EAR
1$ PER EAR

CORN
$1.00
EAR

IT SOUNDS LIKE "PIRATE"
CORN

"A BUCKANEER" $1.00

IN THE WINTER WE HAVE "INDIAN
SNOW" APACHE HERE, APACHE THERE

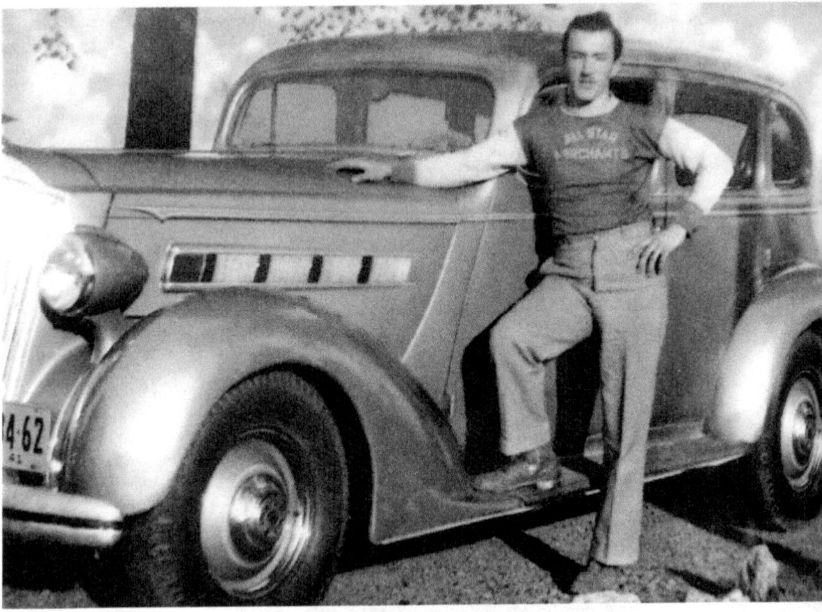

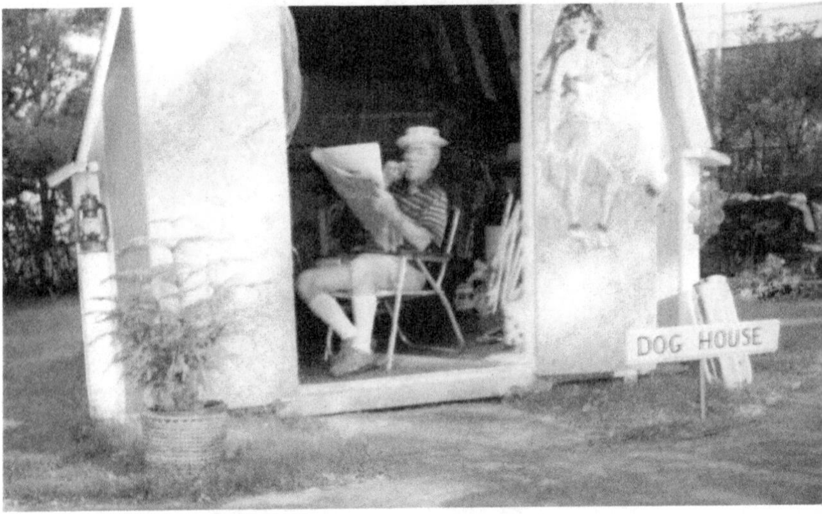
DOG HOUSE

Dad in the Dog House

~~Share your idea of what makes a good friend.~~

FUN! FUN! FUN!

When I was a boy living on Fillmore Ave, When the Circus came to town, My Dad would take me down to the Rail Road and watch them unload the Elephants, Giraffs, Zebras, etc, They had to walk to the Circus Grounds at Broadway + Bailey

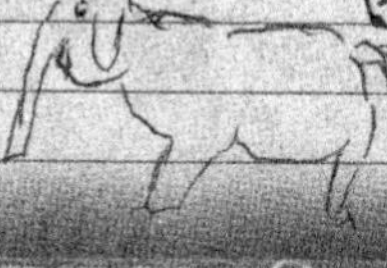

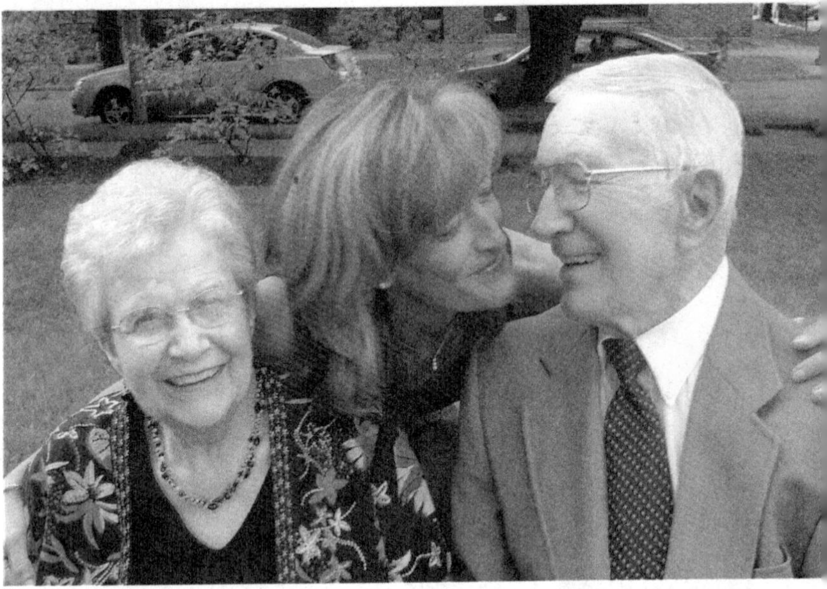

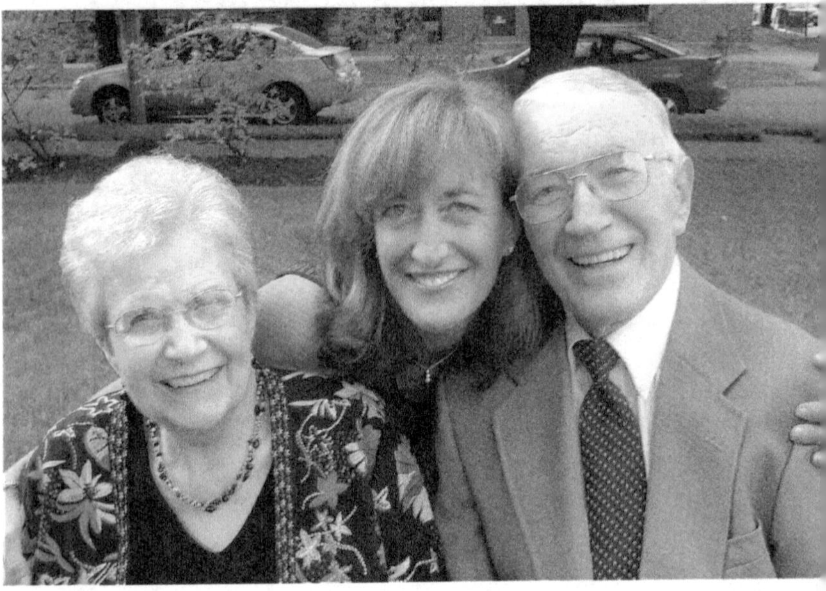

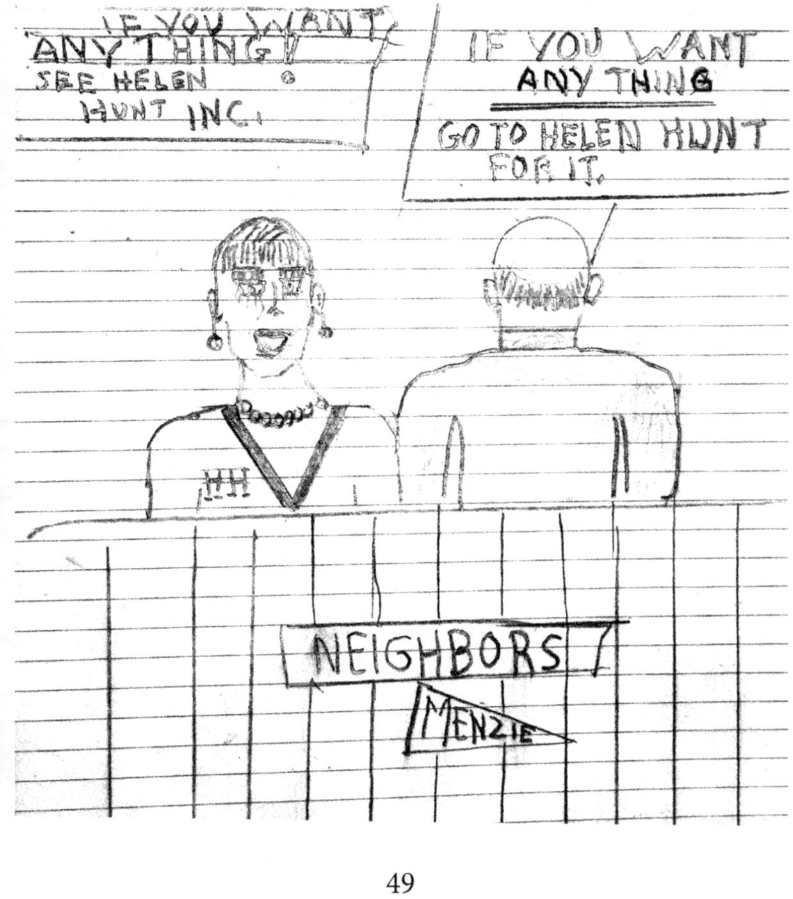
IF YOU WANT ANYTHING!
SEE HELEN HUNT INC.
IF YOU WANT ANY THING
GO TO HELEN HUNT FOR IT.
HH
NEIGHBORS
MENZIE

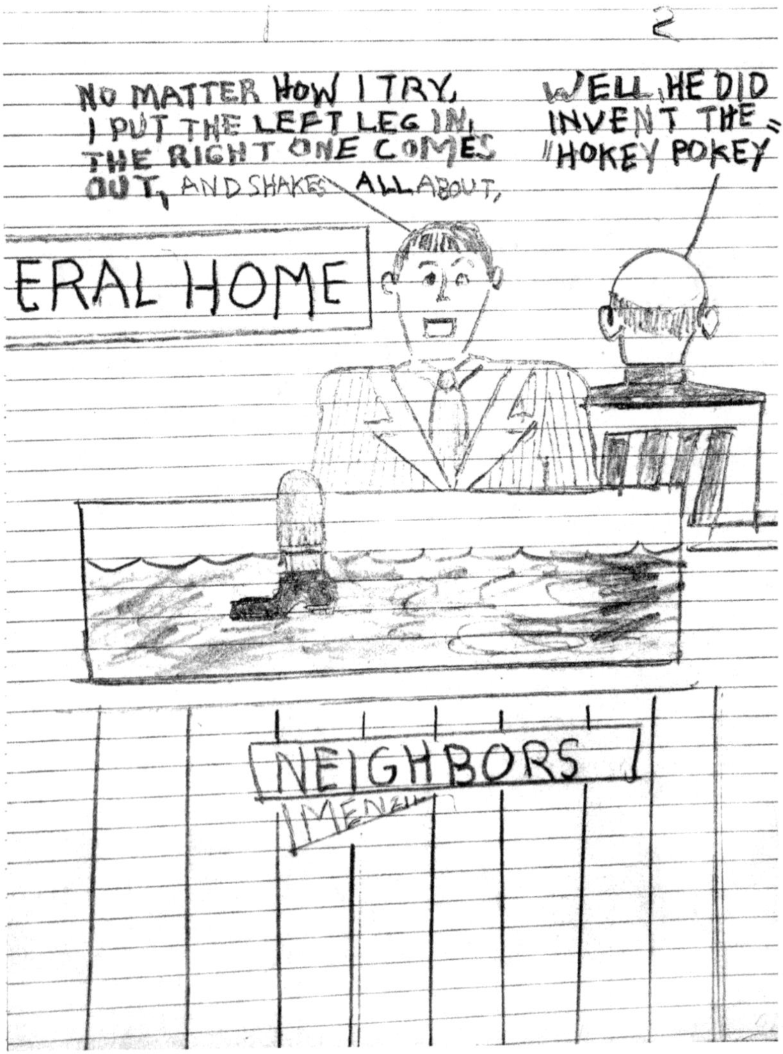
NO MATTER HOW I TRY, I PUT THE LEFT LEG IN, THE RIGHT ONE COMES OUT, AND SHAKES ALL ABOUT,
WELL, HE DID INVENT THE "HOKEY POKEY"
ERAL HOME
NEIGHBORS

SARA, SARA, SITTEN IN A SHOE SHINE SHOP
OH, SHE SHINES + SITS, SITS + SHINES, SHINES + SITS,
SITS + SHINES, SHINES + SITS, SITS + SHINES

SAY IT, START SLOW, THEN FASTER

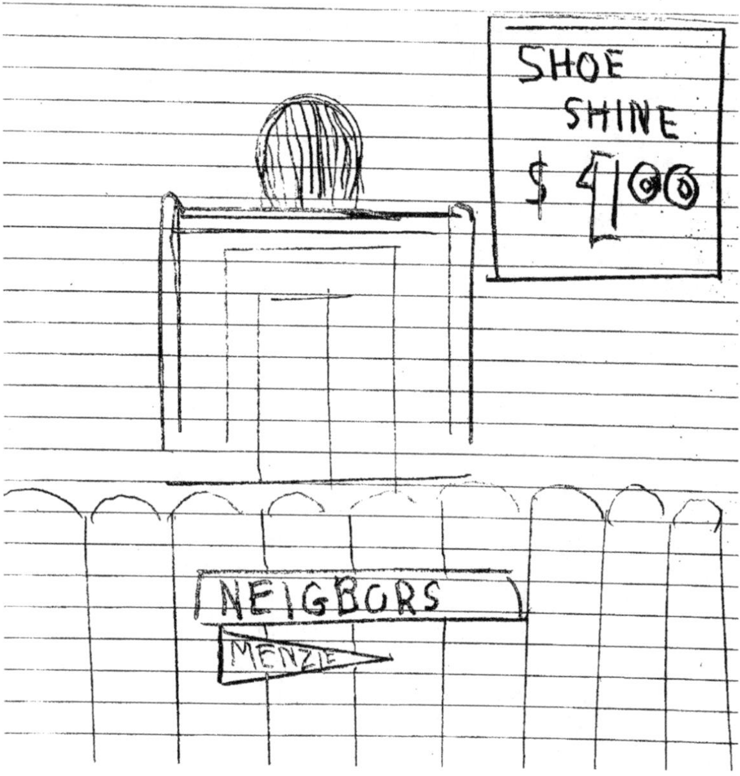
SHOE
SHINE
$100
NEIGBORS
MENZIE

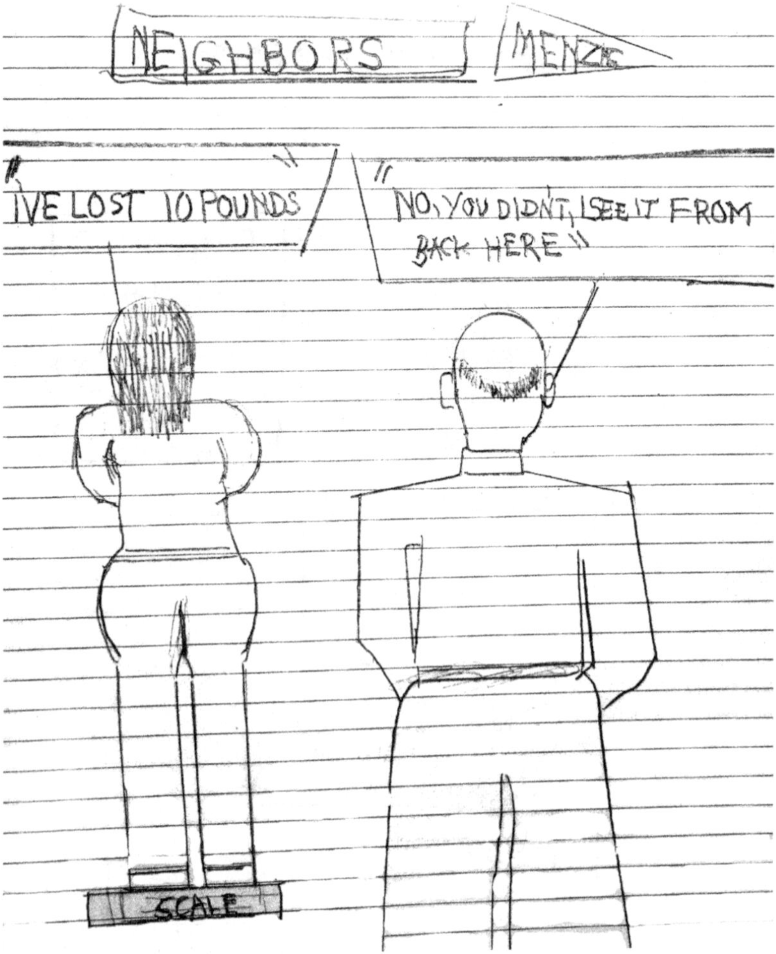
NEIGHBORS
MENZIE
"I'VE LOST 10 POUNDS"
"NO, YOU DIDN'T, I SEE IT FROM BACK HERE"
SCALE

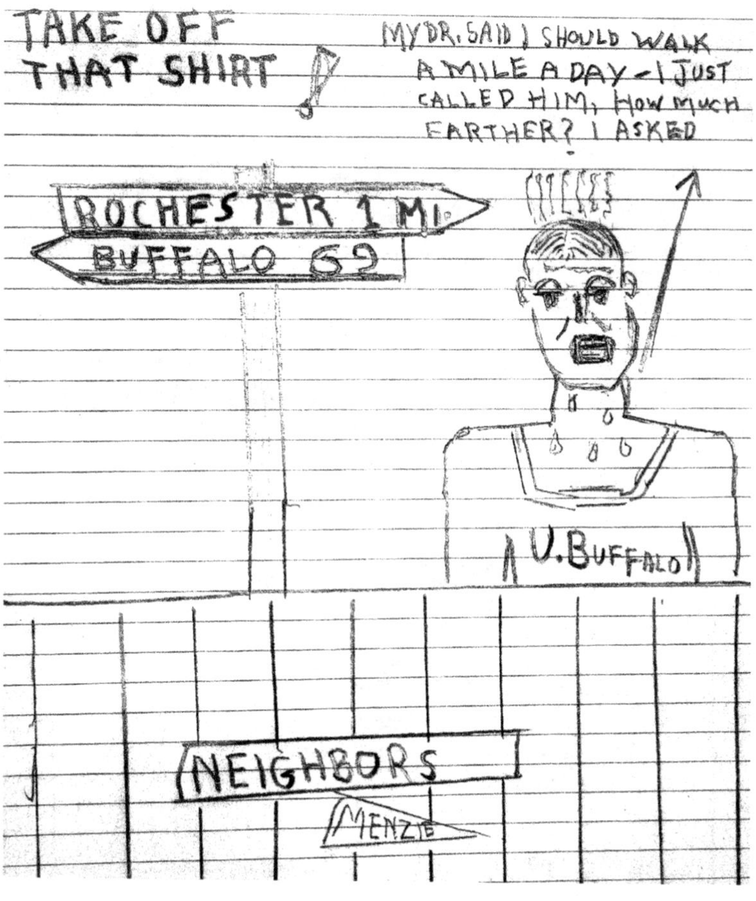
TAKE OFF THAT SHIRT!
MY DR. SAID I SHOULD WALK A MILE A DAY - I JUST CALLED HIM, HOW MUCH FARTHER? I ASKED
ROCHESTER 1 MI.
BUFFALO 69
U. BUFFALO
NEIGHBORS
MENZIE

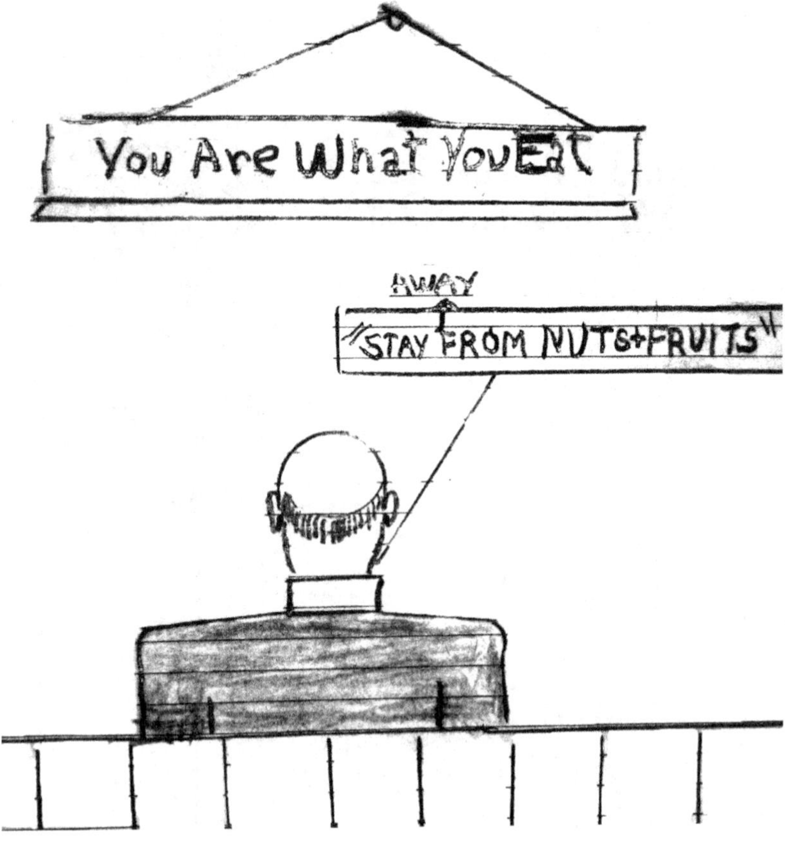
You Are What You Eat
AWAY
"STAY FROM NUTS+FRUITS"

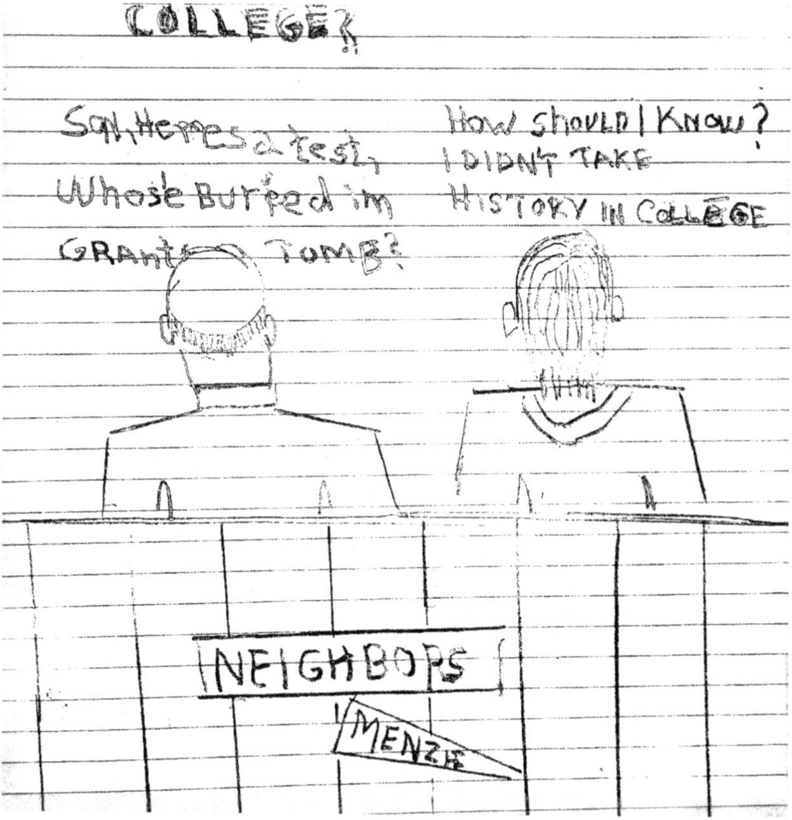
COLLEGE?
Say, Heres a test, Whose Buried in GRANTS TOMB?
How should I Know? I DIDN'T TAKE HISTORY IN COLLEGE
NEIGHBORS
MENZIE

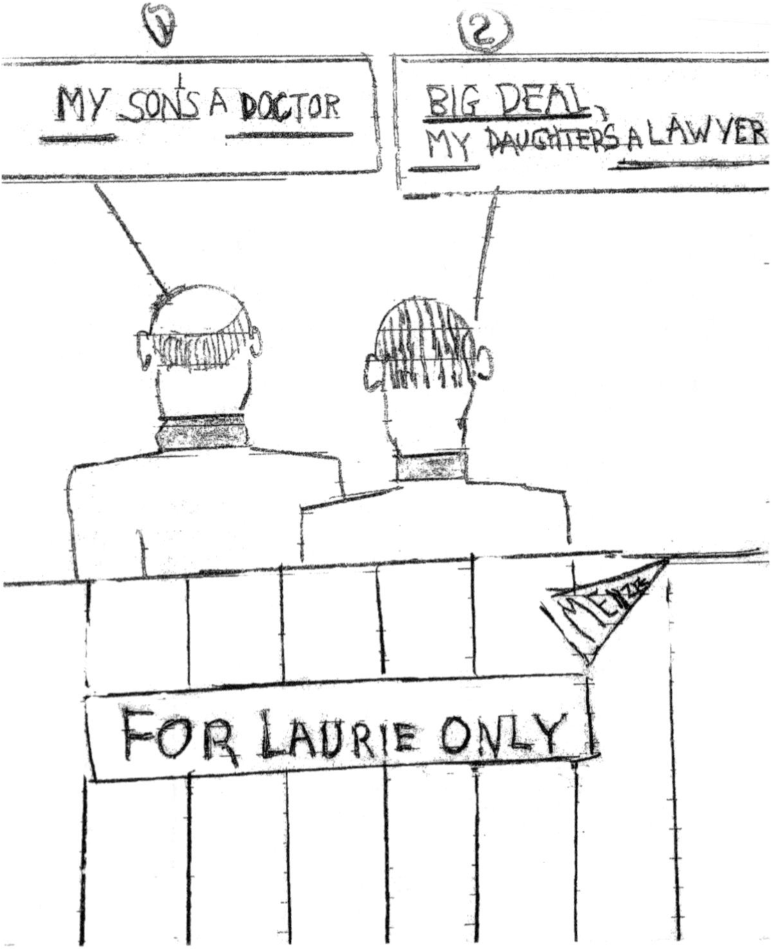
1
MY SON'S A DOCTOR
2
BIG DEAL, MY DAUGHTERS A LAWYER
FOR LAURIE ONLY

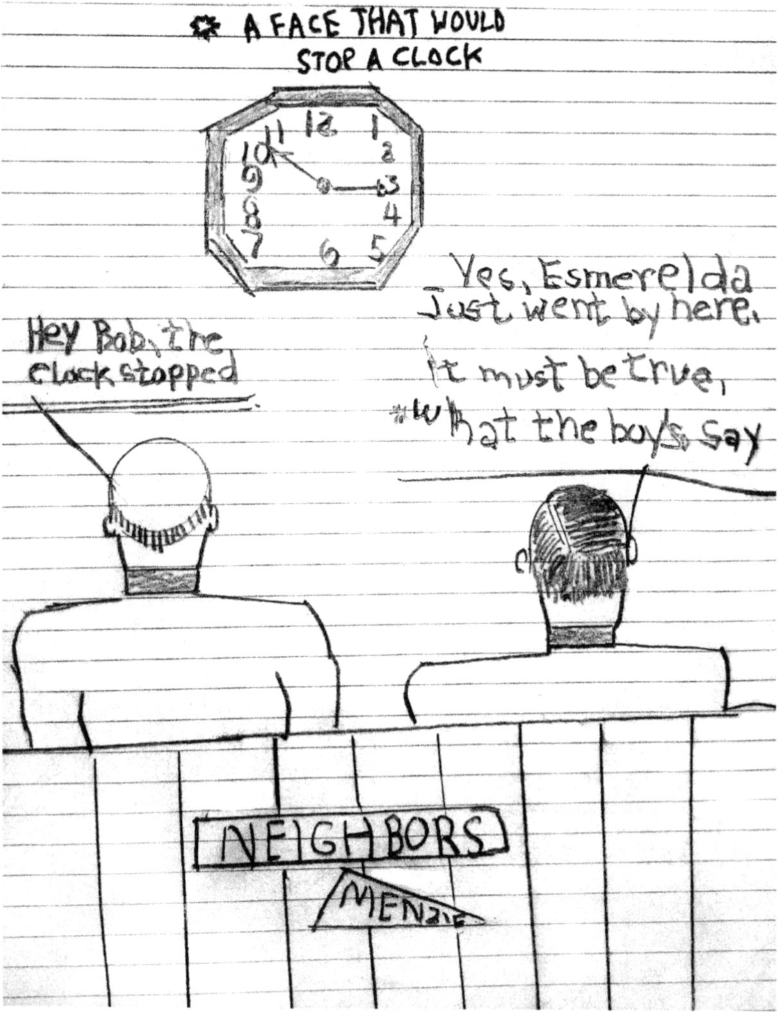

A FACE THAT WOULD STOP A CLOCK
Hey Bob, the clock stopped
Yes, Esmerelda Just went by here. It must be true, what the boys say
NEIGHBORS
MEN

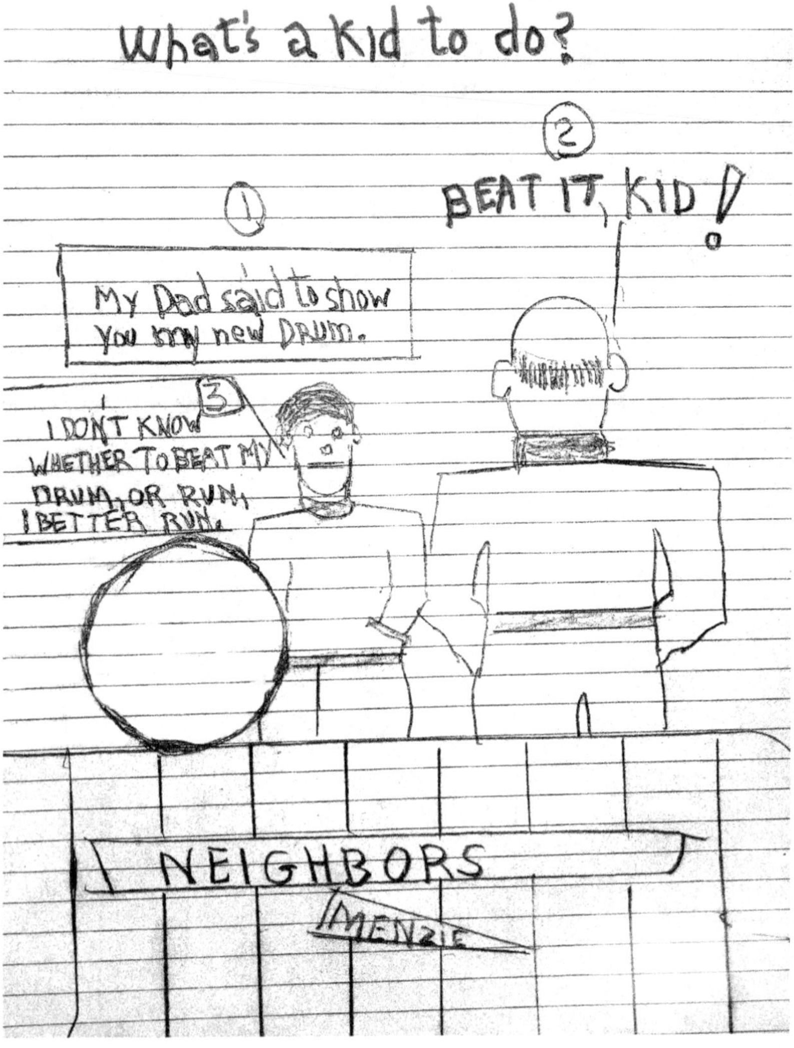

What's a Kid to do?
1
My Dad said to show you my new DRUM.
2
BEAT IT, KID!
3
I DON'T KNOW WHETHER TO BEAT MY DRUM, OR RUN, I BETTER RUN.
NEIGHBORS
MENZIE

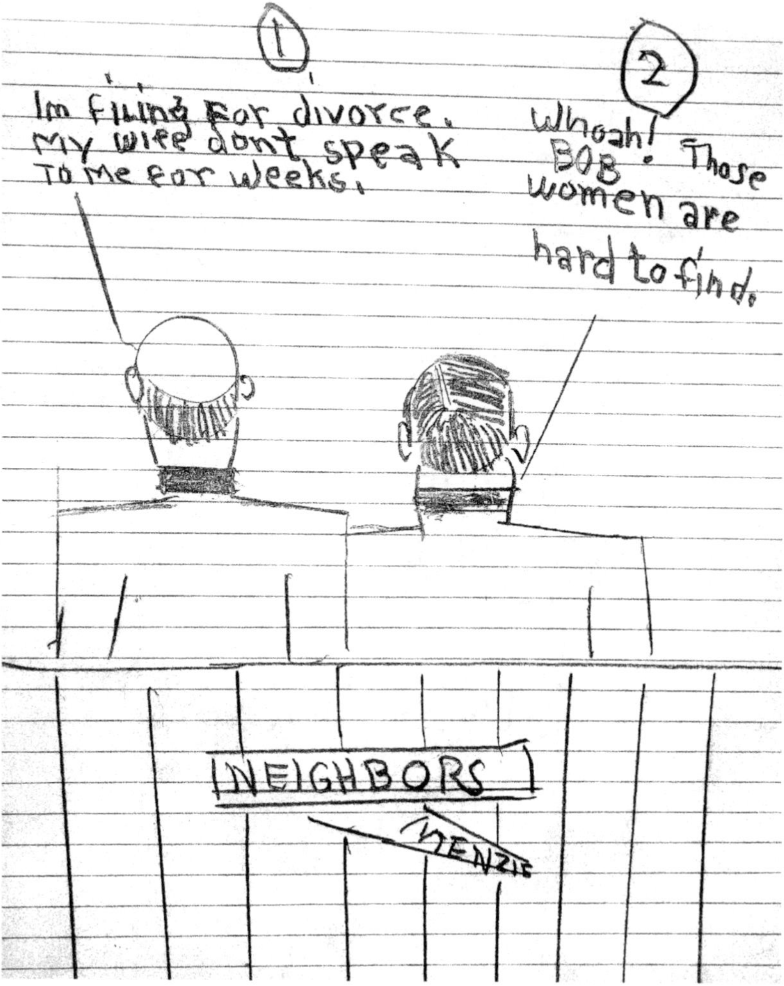
1
Im filing for divorce. my wife dont speak To me for weeks.
2
Whoah! BOB. Those women are hard to find.
NEIGHBORS
KENZIE

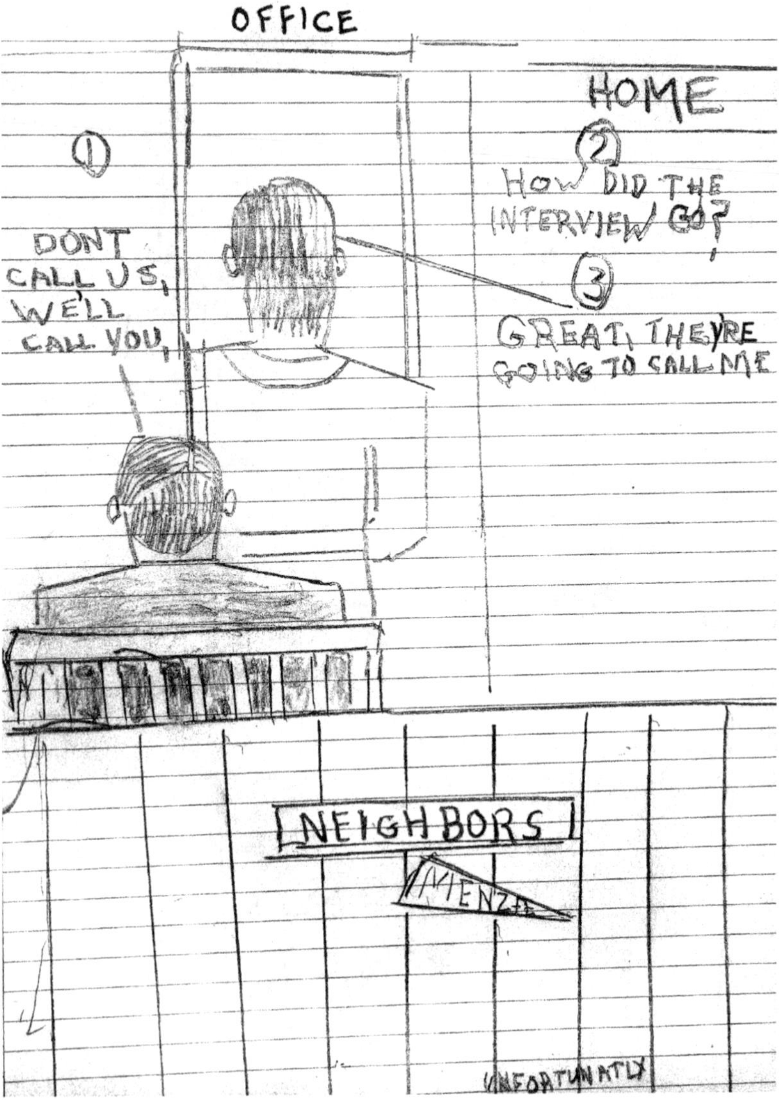
OFFICE
HOME
1
DONT CALL US, WE'LL CALL YOU,
2
HOW DID THE INTERVIEW GO?
3
GREAT, THEY'RE GOING TO CALL ME
NEIGHBORS
MENZIE
UNFORTUNATLY

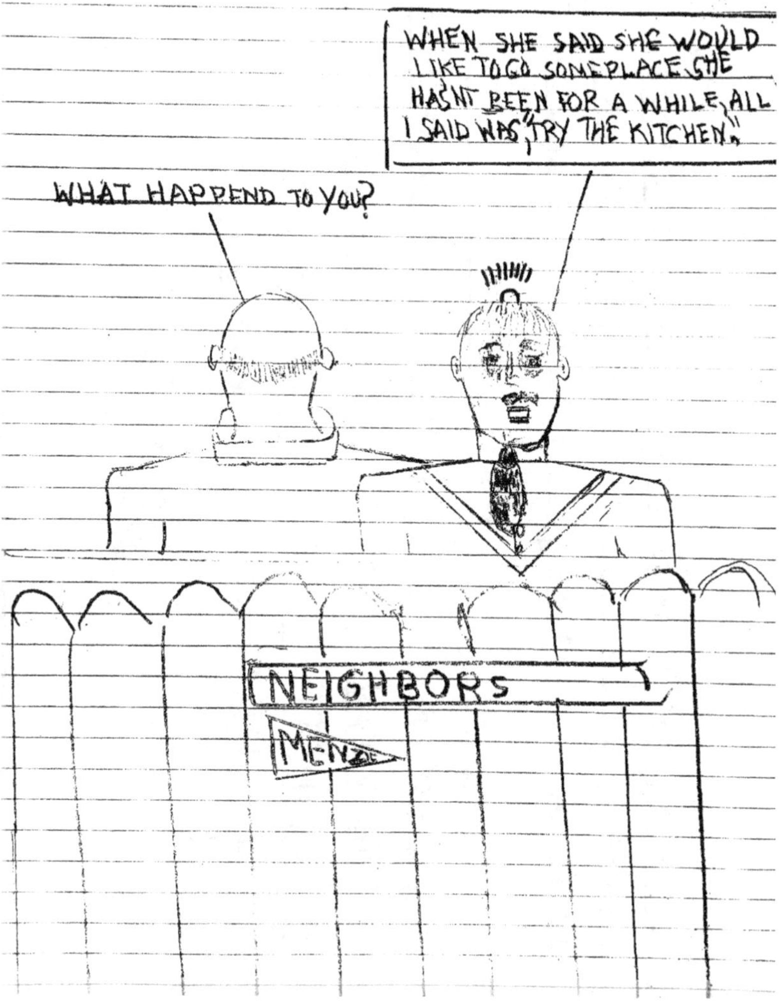
WHEN SHE SAID SHE WOULD LIKE TO GO SOMEPLACE SHE HASN'T BEEN FOR A WHILE, ALL I SAID WAS, "TRY THE KITCHEN."
WHAT HAPPEND TO YOU?
NEIGHBORS
MENZIE

YOU KNOW SUSAN PALIN, JOE'S WIFE, SHE'S BEEN MARRIED 3 TIMES BEFORE. SHE SAID SHE PLANNED IT THAT WAY. NOTE JOE IS THE LOCAL FUNERAL DIRECTOR

| | | |
|---|---|---|
| 1 | BANKER → | ONE FOR THE MONEY |
| 2 | SHOW MAN, M.C. → | TWO FOR THE SHOW |
| 3 | MINISTER → | THREE TO GET READY |
| 4 | UNDERTAKER | FOUR TO GO |

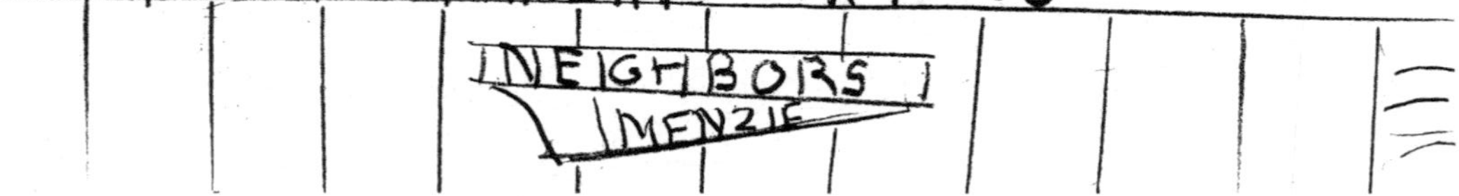
NEIGHBORS
MENZIE

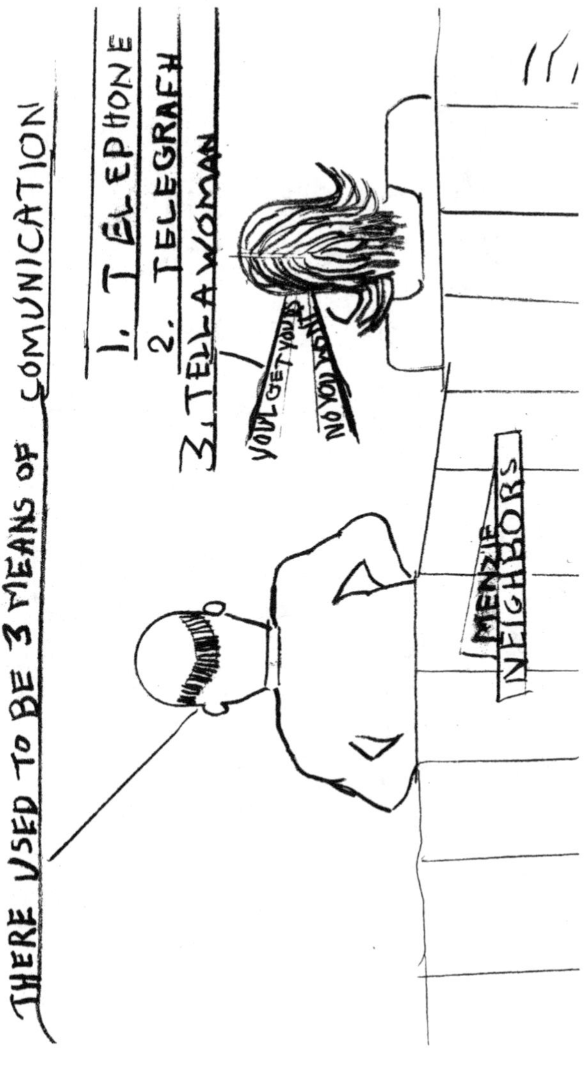
THERE USED TO BE 3 MEANS OF COMUNICATION
1. TELEPHONE
2. TELEGRAPH
3. TELL A WOMAN
YOU'LL GET YOURS
MENZIE
NEIGHBORS

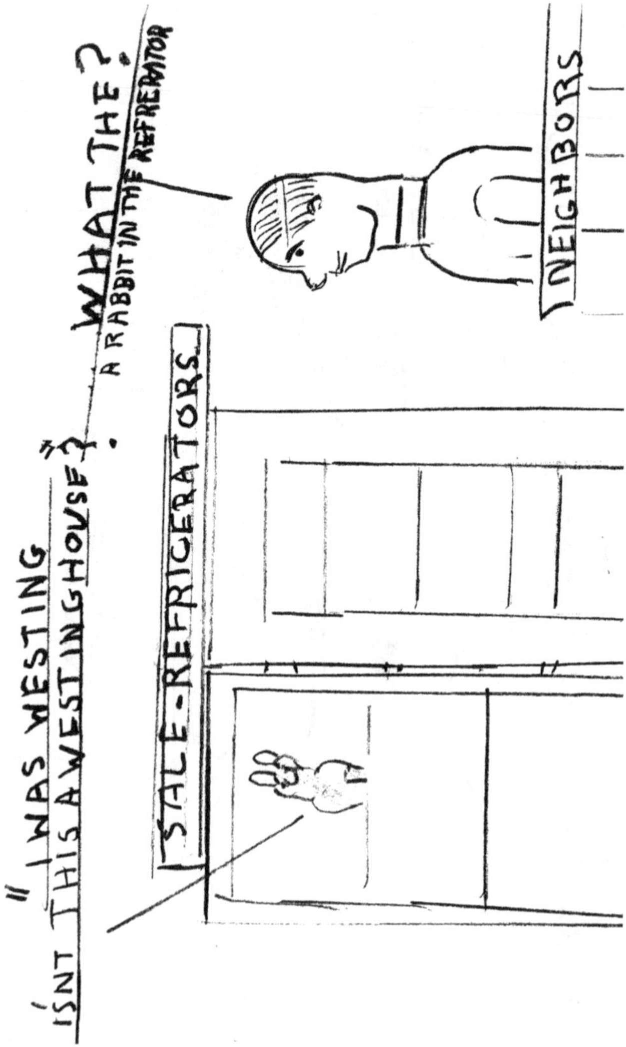
"I WAS WESTING"
ISN'T THIS A WESTINGHOUSE?
WHAT THE?
A RABBIT IN THE REFRERATOR
SALE - REFRIGERATORS
NEIGHBORS

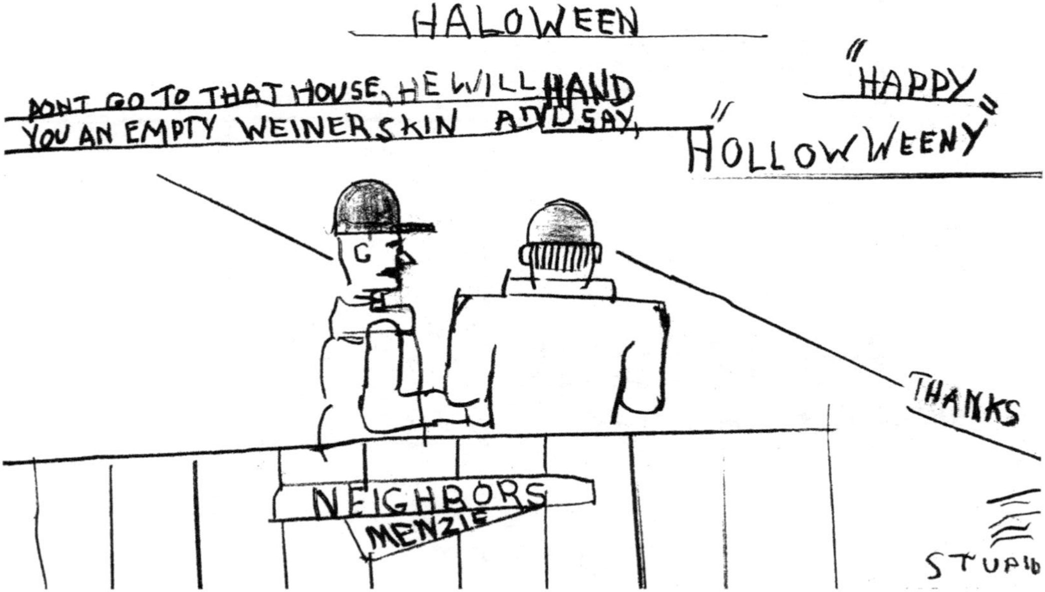
HALOWEEN
DONT GO TO THAT HOUSE, HE WILL HAND YOU AN EMPTY WEINER SKIN AND SAY,
"HAPPY "HOLLOW WEENY"
THANKS
NEIGHBORS
MENZIE
STUPID

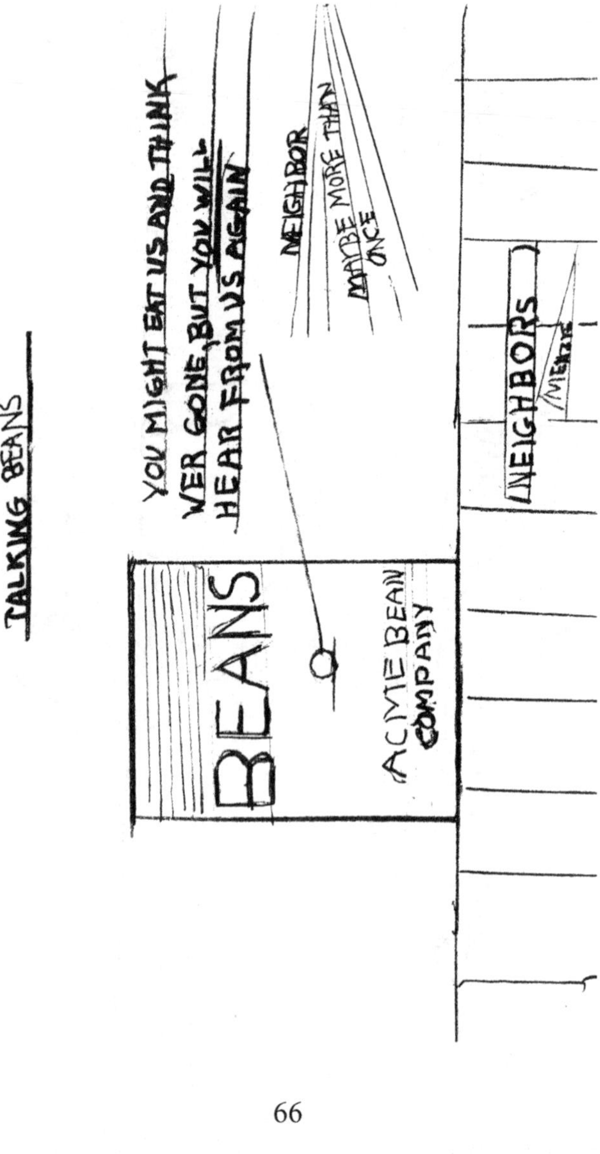
TALKING BEANS
YOU MIGHT EAT US AND THINK
VER GONE, BUT YOU WILL
HEAR FROM US AGAIN
NEIGHBOR
MAYBE MORE THAN
ONCE
NEIGHBORS
BEANS
ACME BEAN
COMPANY

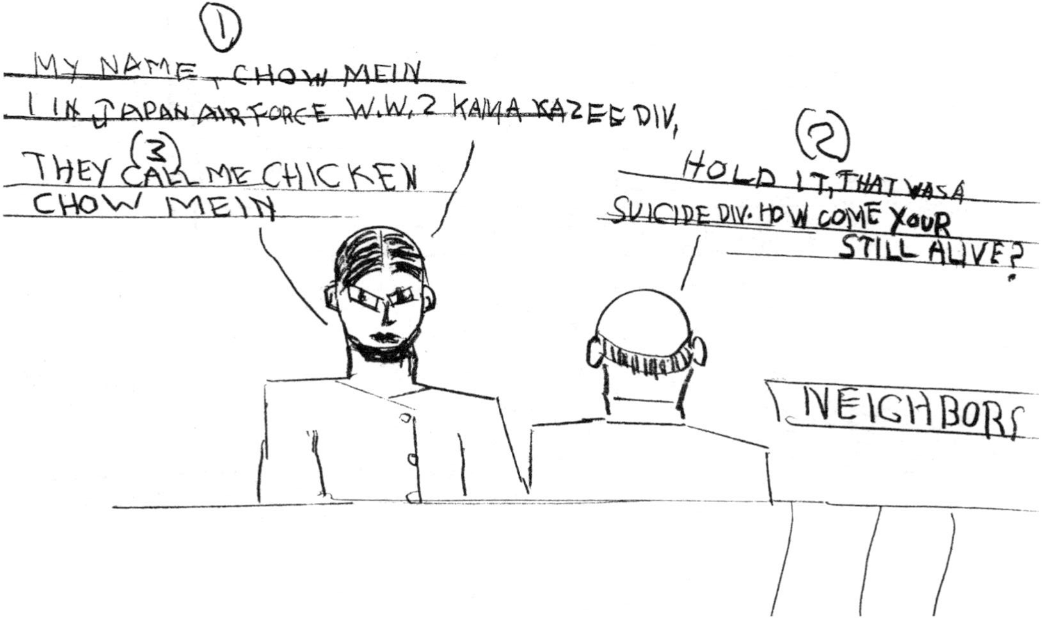
1
MY NAME, CHOW MEIN
I IN JAPAN AIR FORCE W.W.2 KAMA KAZEE DIV,
2
HOLD IT, THAT WAS A SUICIDE DIV. HOW COME YOUR STILL ALIVE?
3
THEY CALL ME CHICKEN CHOW MEIN
NEIGHBORS

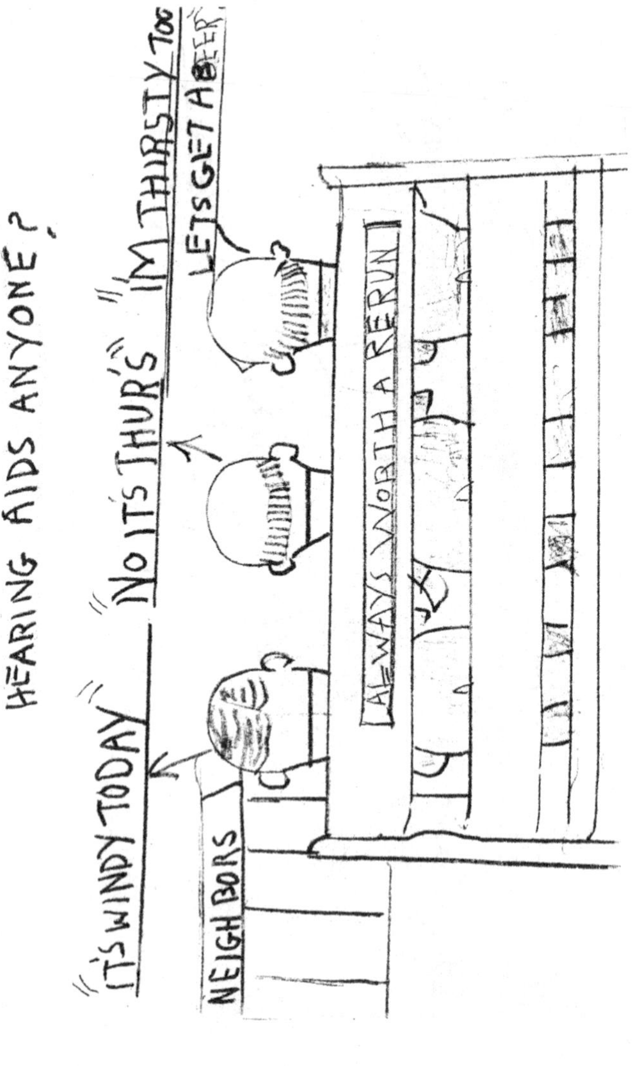
HEARING AIDS ANYONE?
IT'S WINDY TODAY
NO IT'S THURS
I'M THIRSTY TOO
LETS GET A BEER
ALWAYS WORTH A RERUN
NEIGH BORS

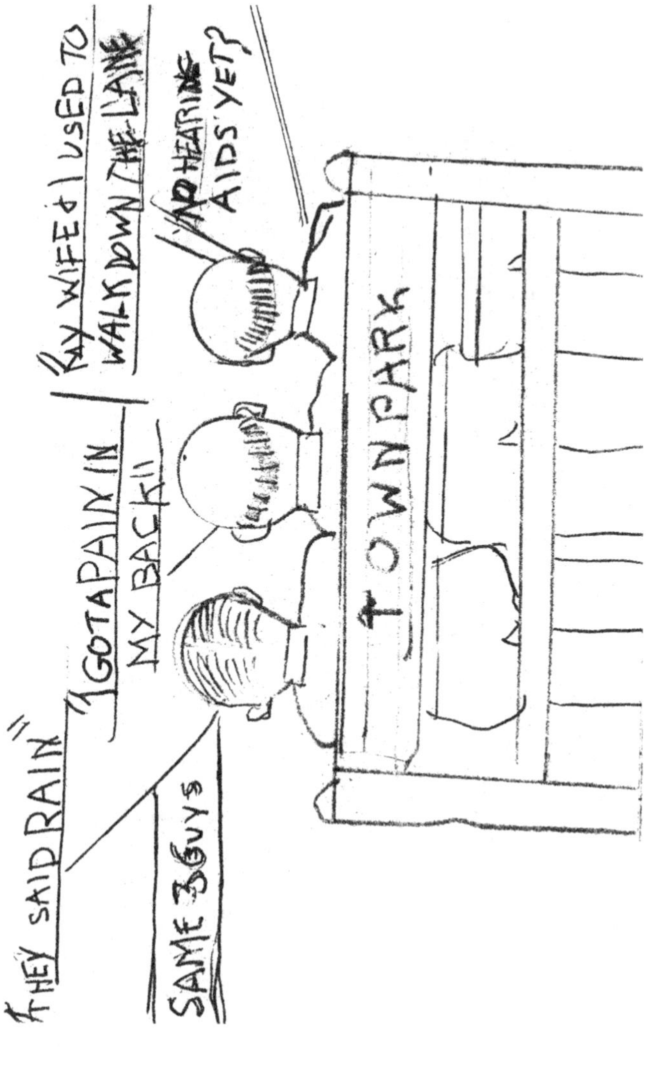

"THEY SAID RAIN"
"I GOT A PAIN IN MY BACK!!
MY WIFE & I USED TO WALK DOWN THE LANE
NO HEARING AIDS YET?
SAME 3 GUYS
TOWN PARK

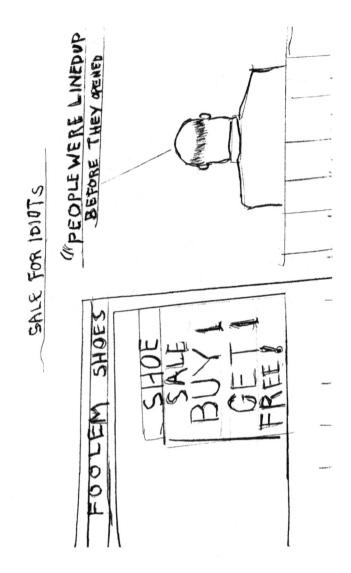

SALE FOR IDIOTS

"PEOPLE WERE LINEDUP BEFORE THEY OPENED"

FOOLEM SHOES

SHOE SALE BUY 1 GET 1 FREE!

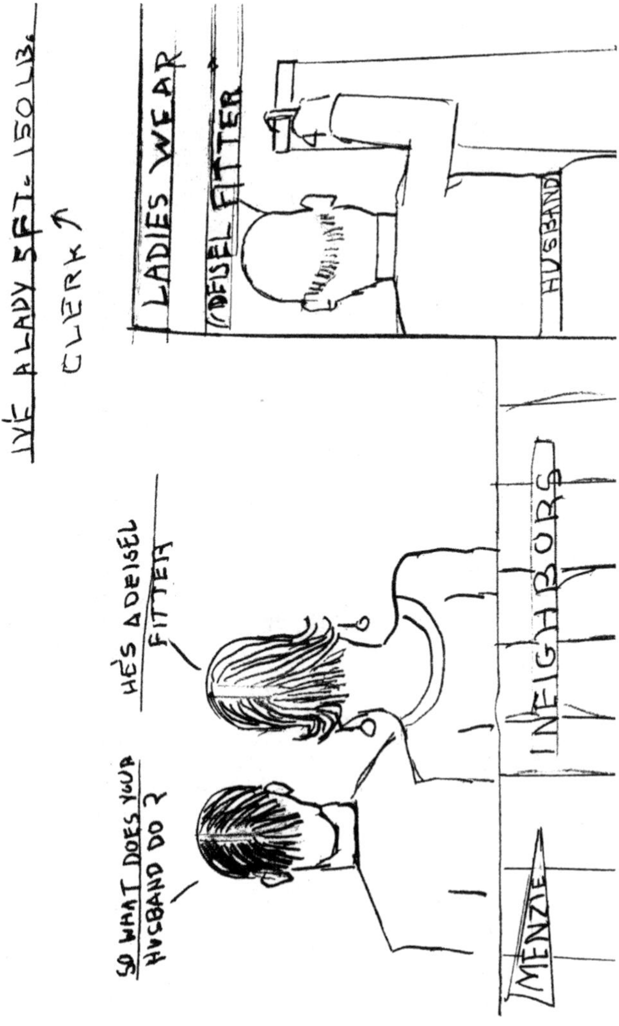
MENZIE
SO WHAT DOES YOUR HUSBAND DO ?
HE'S A DEISEL FITTER
NEIGHBORS
I'VE A LADY 5FT. 150 LB.
CLERK
LADIES WEAR
DEISEL FITTER
HUSBAND

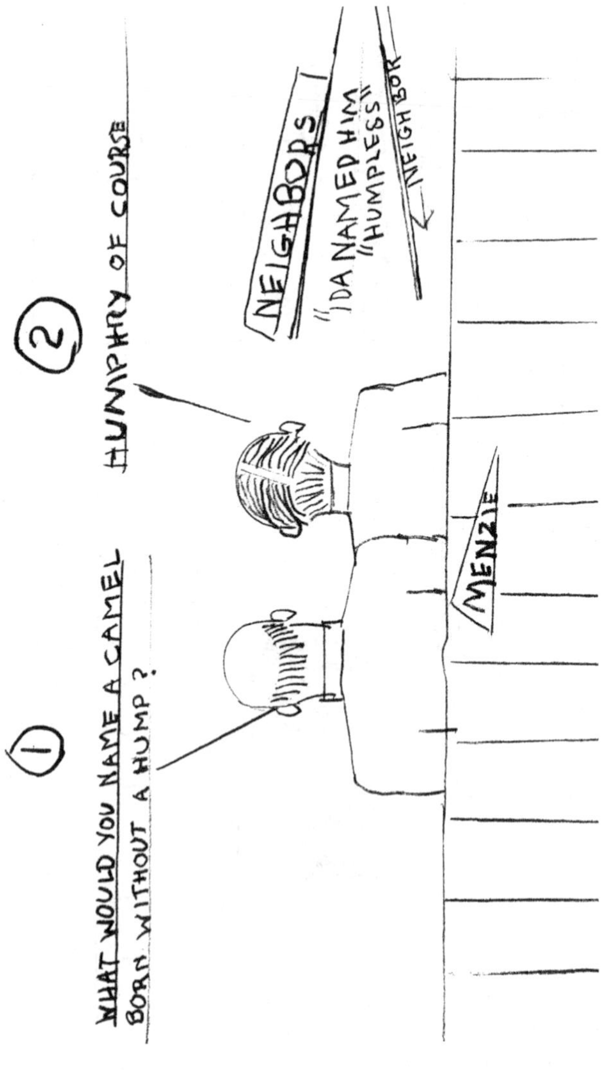
1
WHAT WOULD YOU NAME A CAMEL BORN WITHOUT A HUMP?
2
HUMPHRY OF COURSE
NEIGHBORS
"IDA NAMED HIM "HUMPLESS""
NEIGHBOR
MENZIE

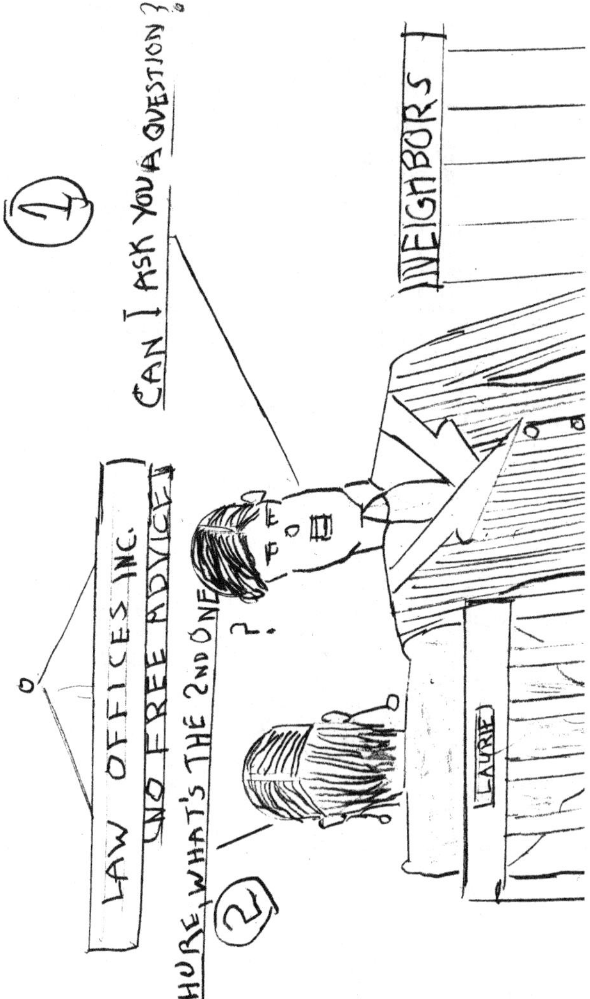
CAN I ASK YOU A QUESTION?
SHURE, WHAT'S THE 2ND ONE
LAW OFFICES INC.
NO FREE ADVICE
NEIGHBORS
LAURIE

IS SHE MARRIED?
MARRIED? SHE'S BEEN MARRIED SO MANY TIMES, SHE'S GOT RICE MARKS ON HER FACE
NEIGHBORS

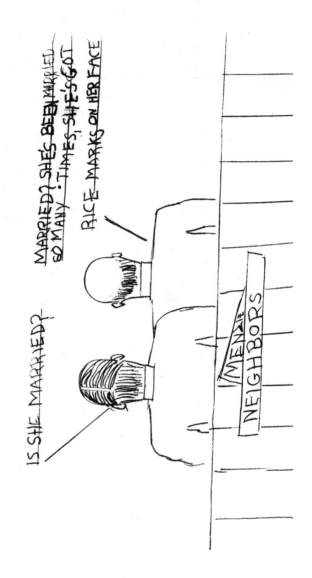

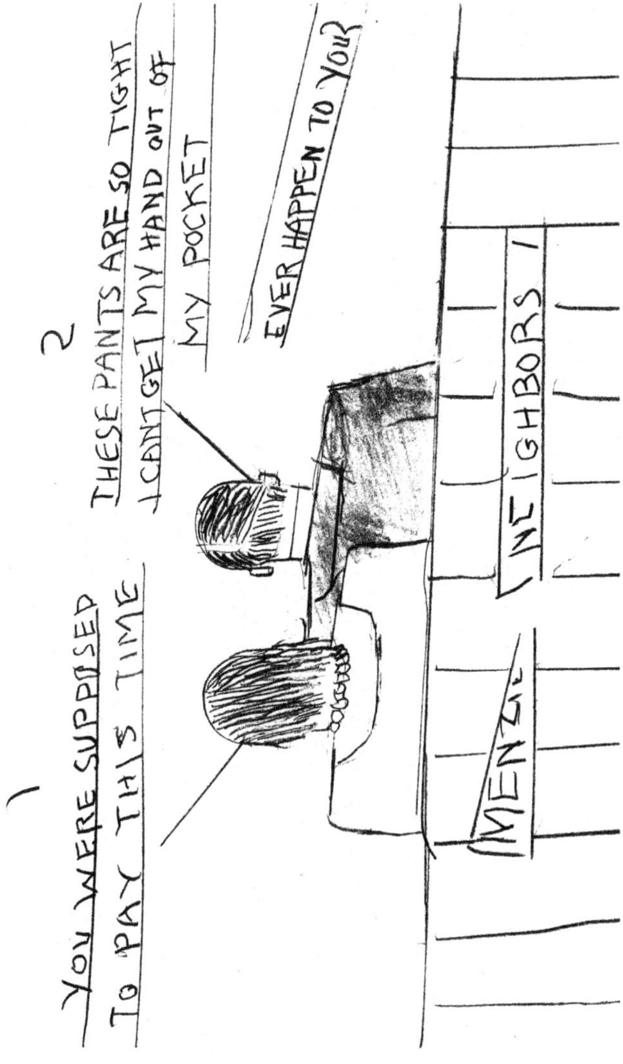
1
YOU WERE SUPPOSED TO PAY THIS TIME
2
THESE PANTS ARE SO TIGHT I CAN'T GET MY HAND OUT OF MY POCKET
EVER HAPPEN TO YOU?
MENZIE NEIGHBORS!

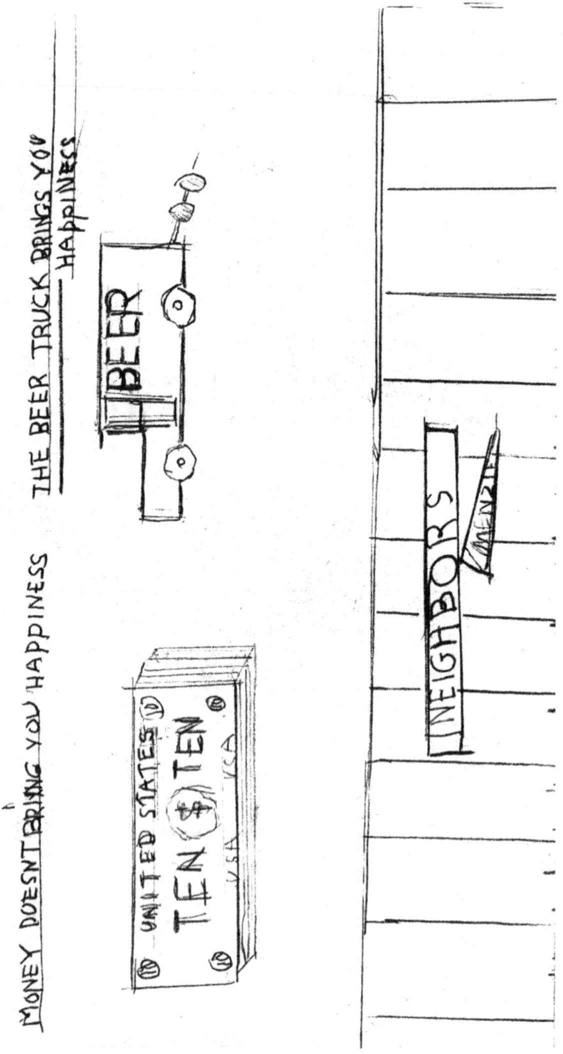
MONEY DOESNT BRING YOU HAPPINESS
THE BEER TRUCK BRINGS YOU HAPPINESS
BEER
UNITED STATES
TEN TEN
NEIGHBORS

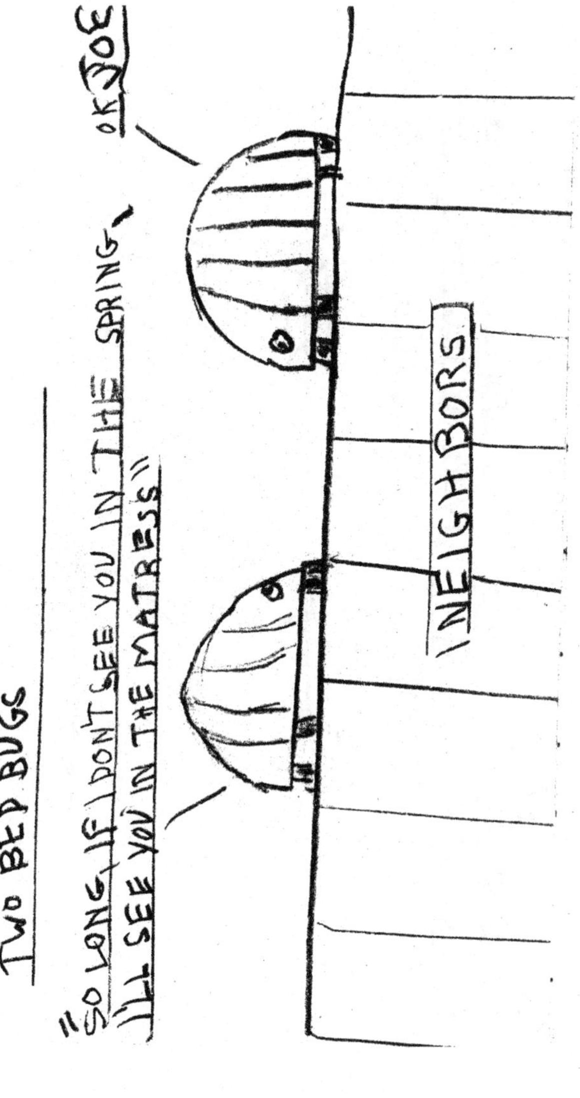
TWO BED BUGS
"SO LONG, IF I DON'T SEE YOU IN THE SPRING,
I'LL SEE YOU IN THE MATRESS"
OK JOE
NEIGHBORS

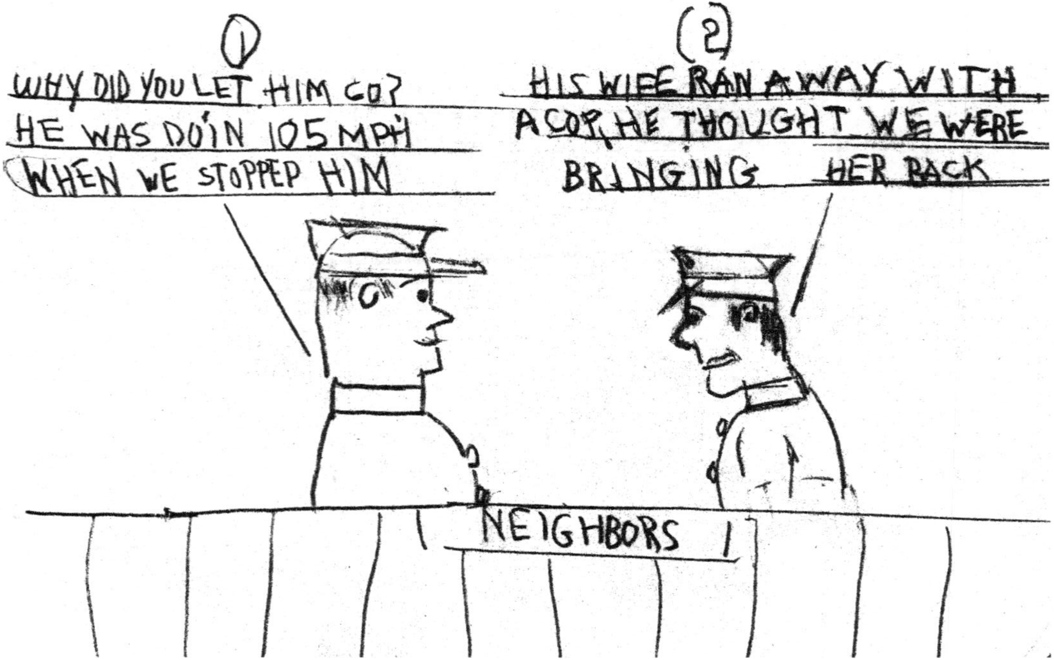

1
WHY DID YOU LET HIM GO?
HE WAS DO'IN 105 MPH
WHEN WE STOPPED HIM
2
HIS WIFE RAN AWAY WITH
A COP, HE THOUGHT WE WERE
BRINGING HER BACK
NEIGHBORS

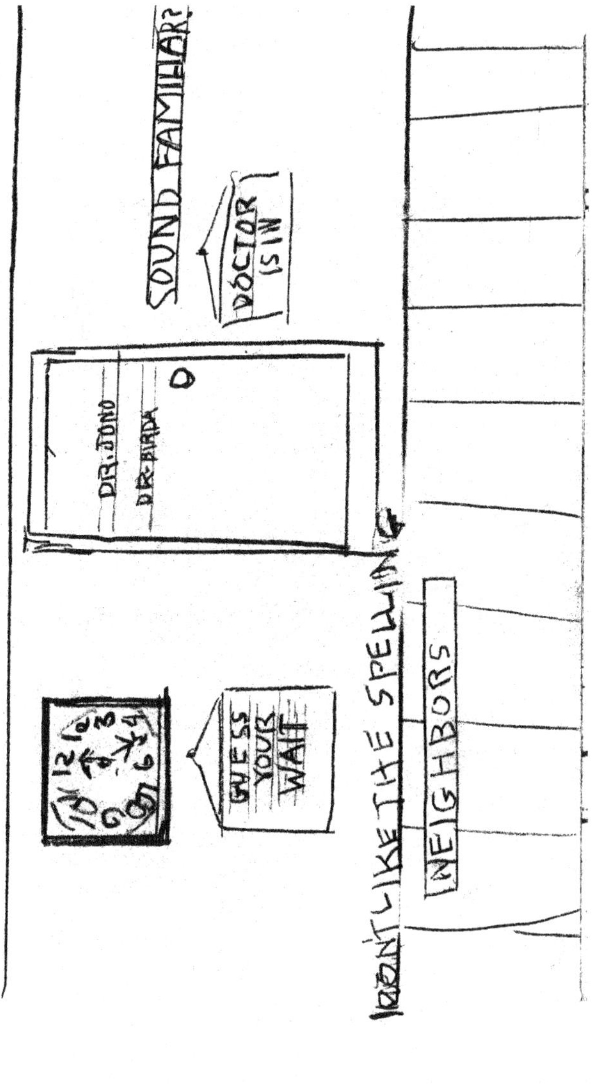
SOUND FAMILIAR?
DOCTOR IS IN
DR. JONO
DR. BIRDA
GUESS YOUR WAIT
I DON'T LIKE THE SPELLING
NEIGHBORS

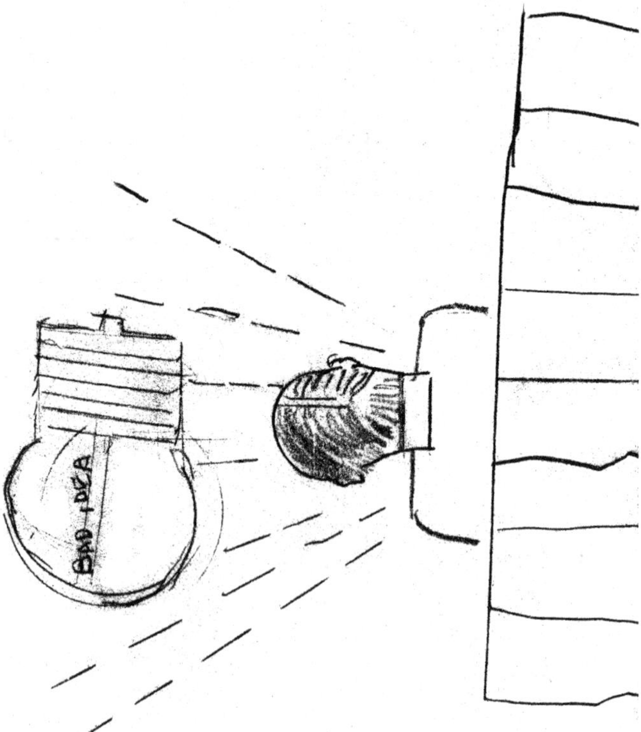
BAD IDEA

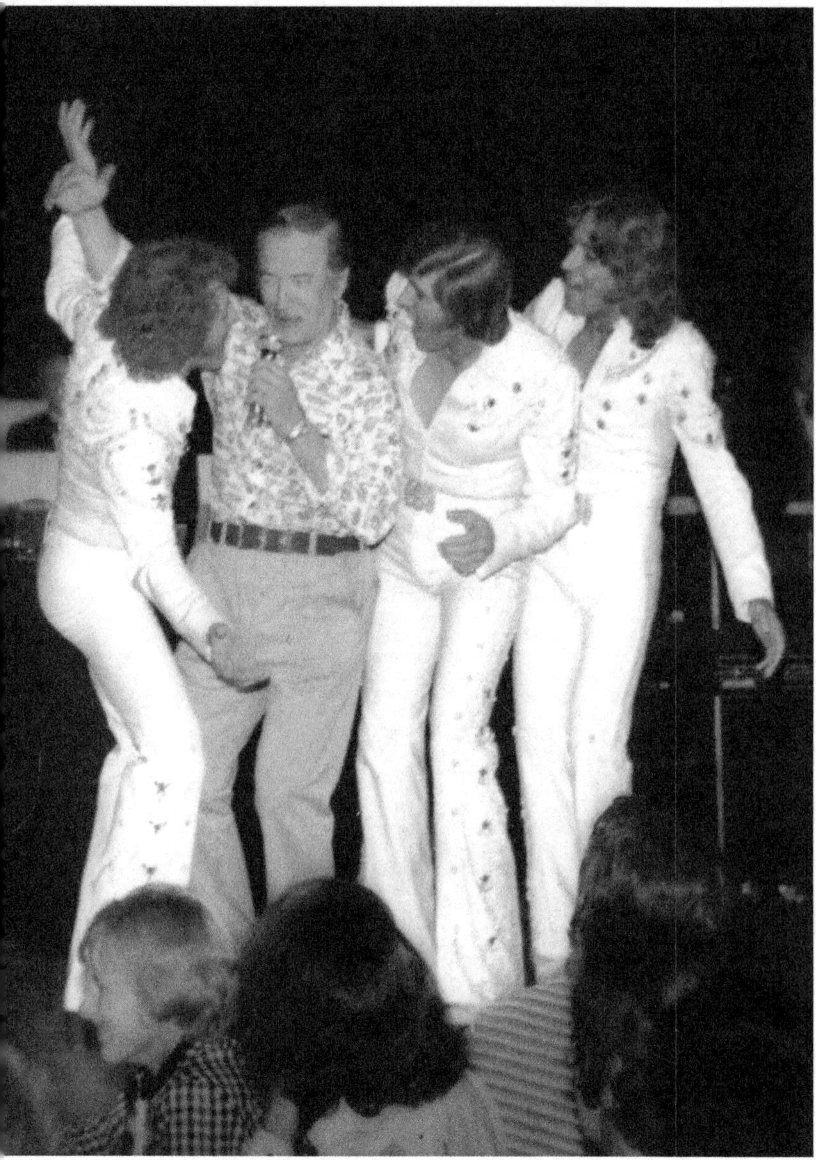

Dad with his back-up singers — The Lettermen
Las Vegas, 1977

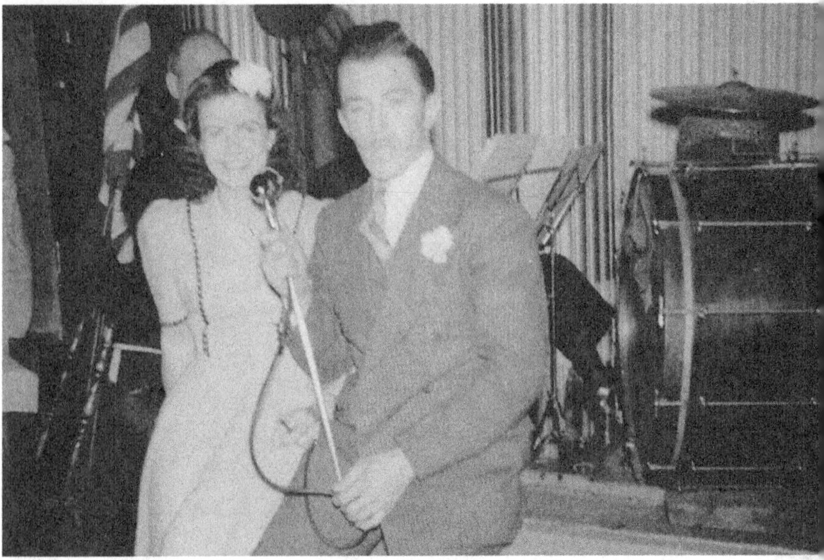

Mom and Dad — 1939

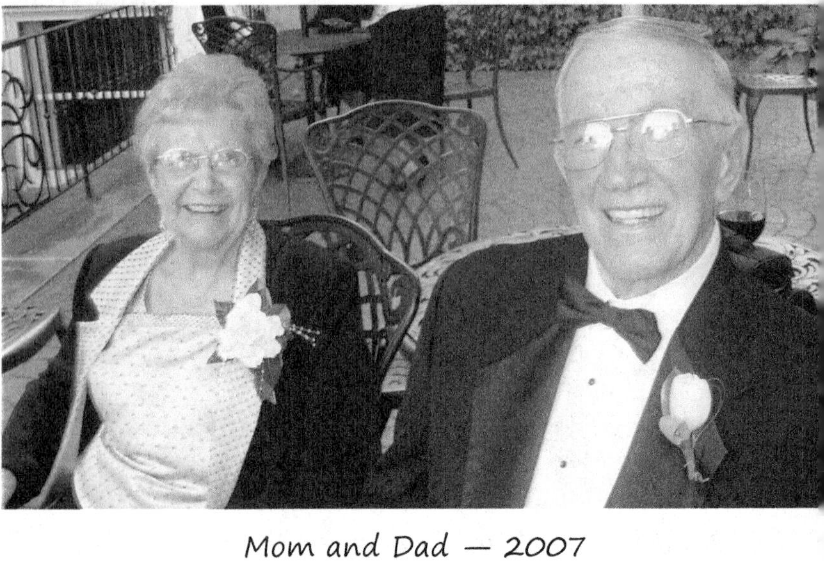

Mom and Dad — 2007

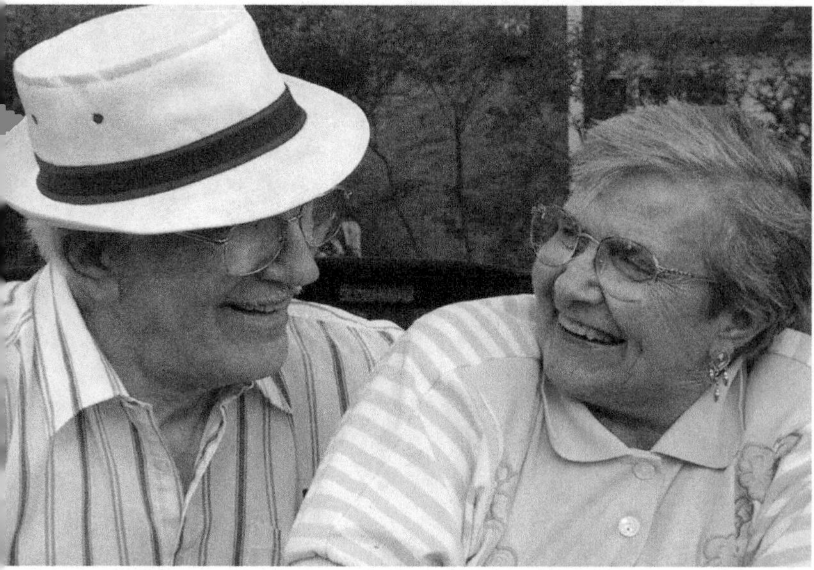

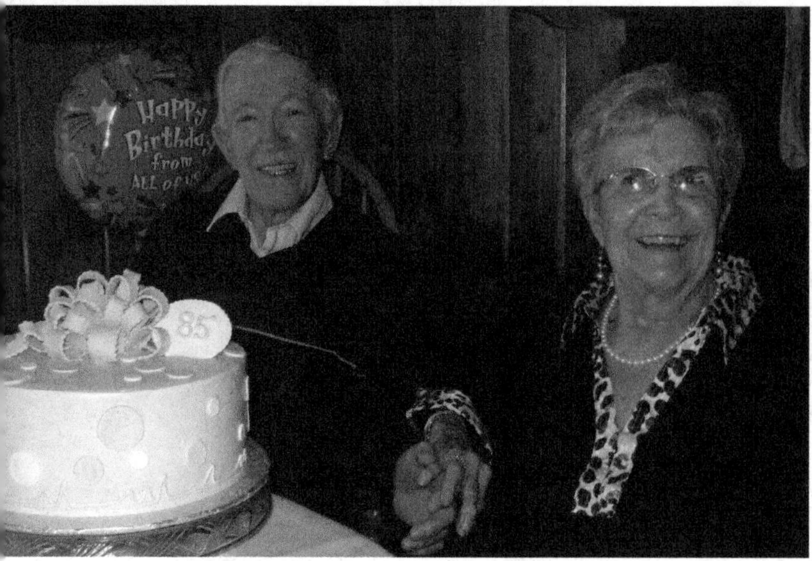
Happy Birthday from ALL of us
85

Mom's $85^{th}$ Birthday (Dad was 92)

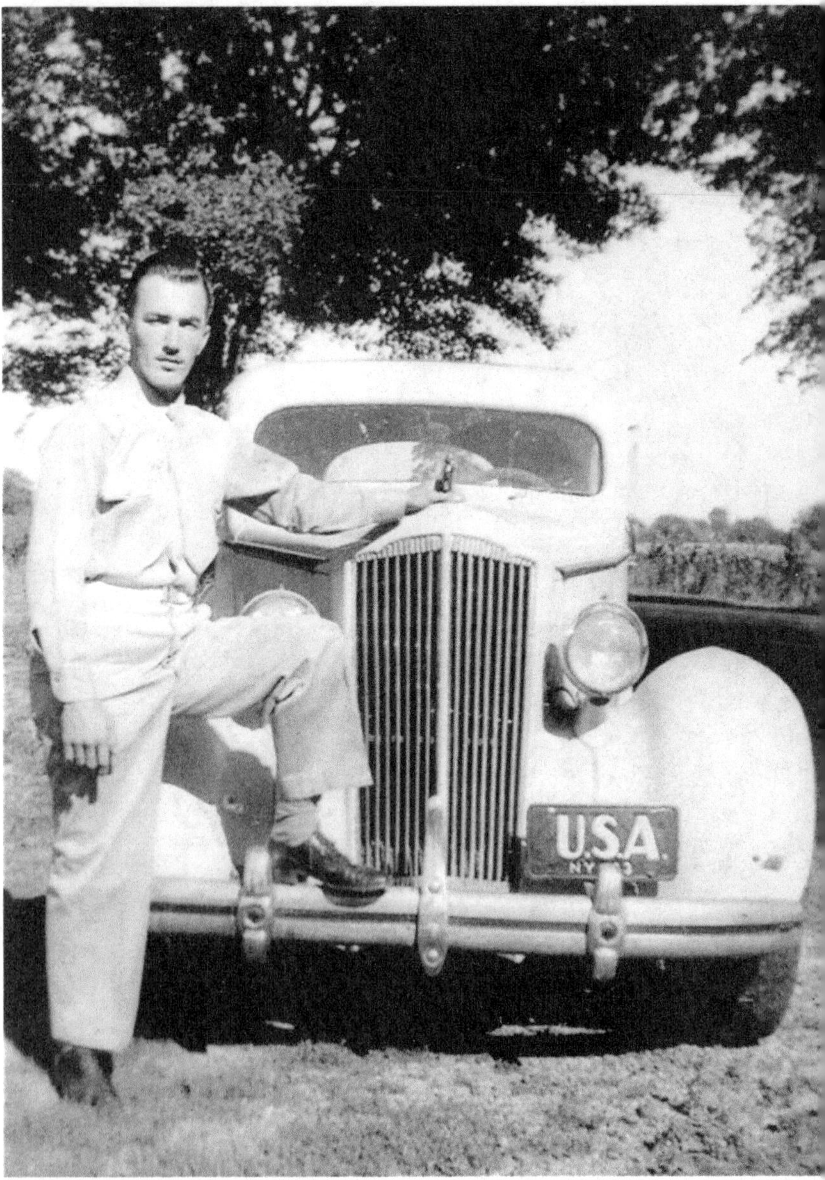
USA

Dad with his 1937 Packard

AUTOMOBILES I HAVE OWNED

CARS

~~What is your favorite memory of your mother? Why is it so special to you?~~

1930 JORDAN

1931 CHRYSLER CONV.

1932 CHEVROLET COUPE

1937 PACKARD

1950 STUDEBAKER

~~1957 GREMLIN~~

1960 AMBASADOR

1964 BUICK CONV.

1969 BUICK LESABRE

1980 " REVIERA

1999 " LESABRE

2006 " LACROSS

2007 " LUCERNE

1976 PACER

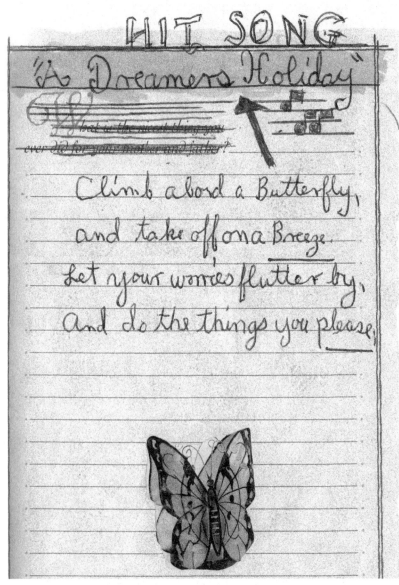

# HIT SONG

## "A Dreamers Holiday"

~~that is the nicest thing you~~
~~ever did for your mother and father?~~

Climb abord a Butterfly,
and take off on a Breeze.
Let your worries flutter by,
And do the things you please.

Dad's Favorite Song: "A Dreamer's Holiday"*
*Music by Mabel Wayne, Lyrics by Kim Gannon — 1949

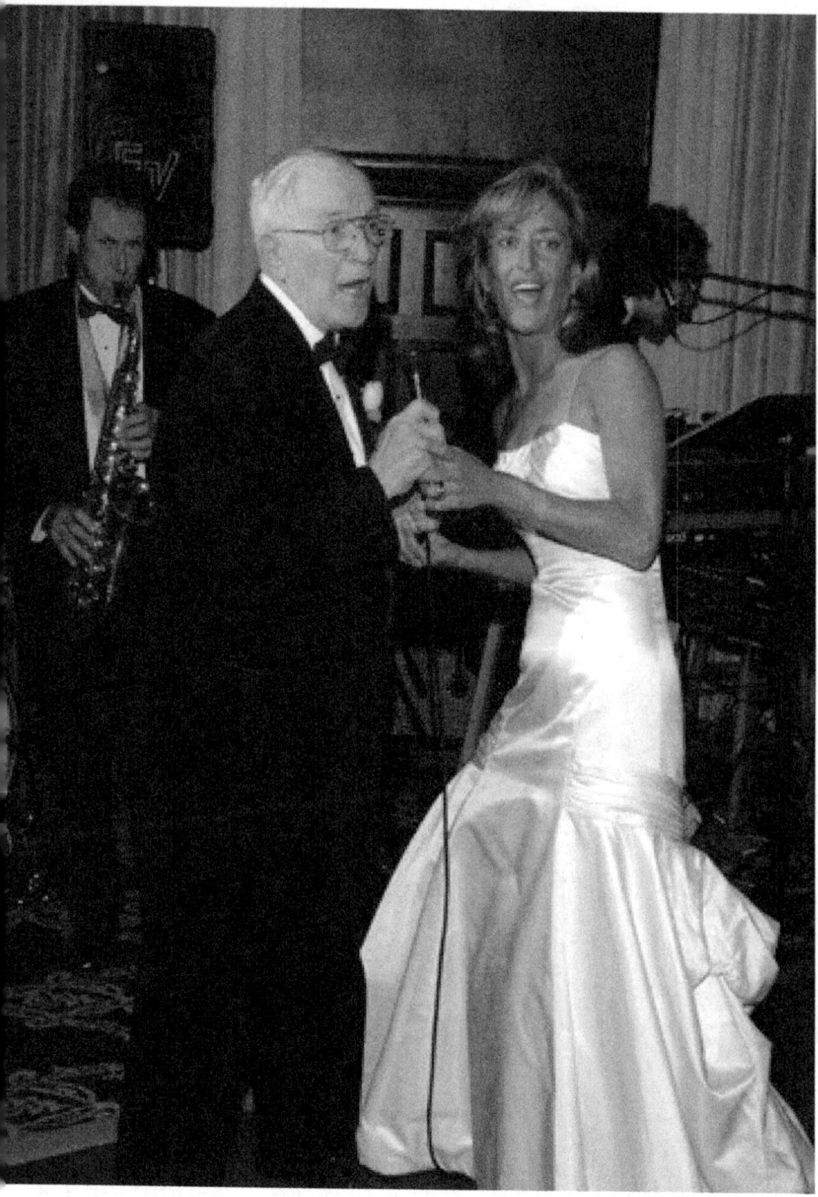

A Dreamer's Holiday

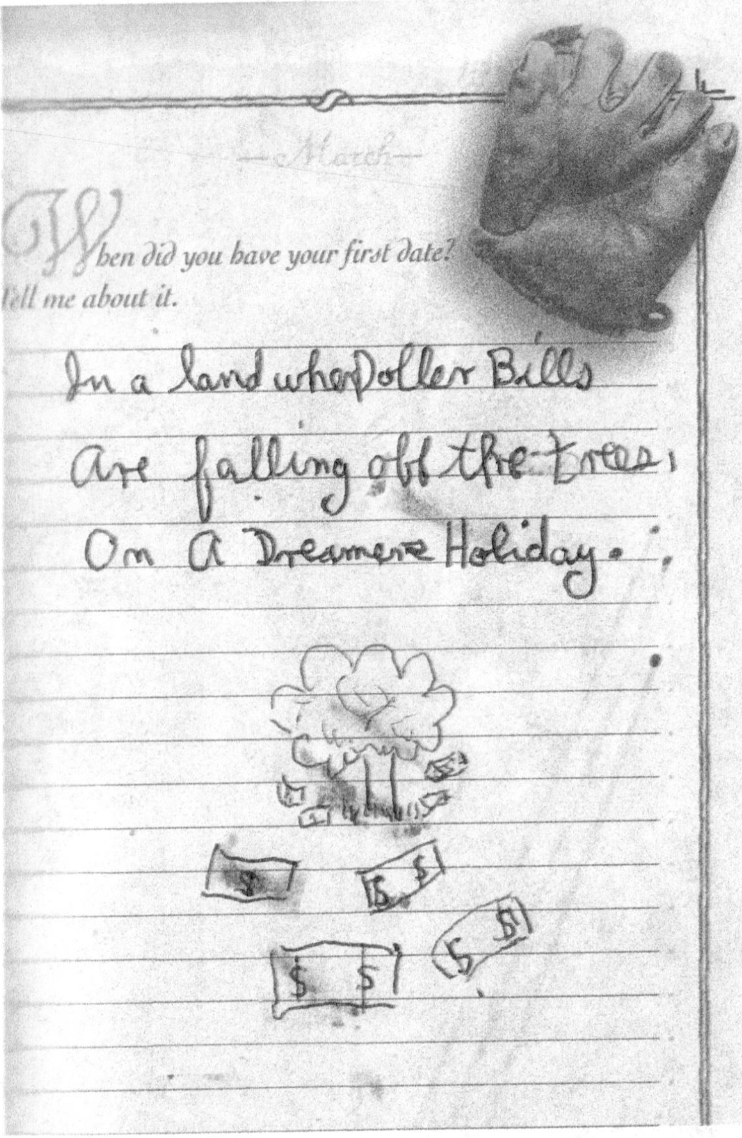
—March—

*When did you have your first date?*
*Tell me about it.*

In a land wherDoller Bills
Are falling off the trees,
On A Dreamere Holiday.

(Dad started ignoring the printed questions and began writing whatever he liked instead.)

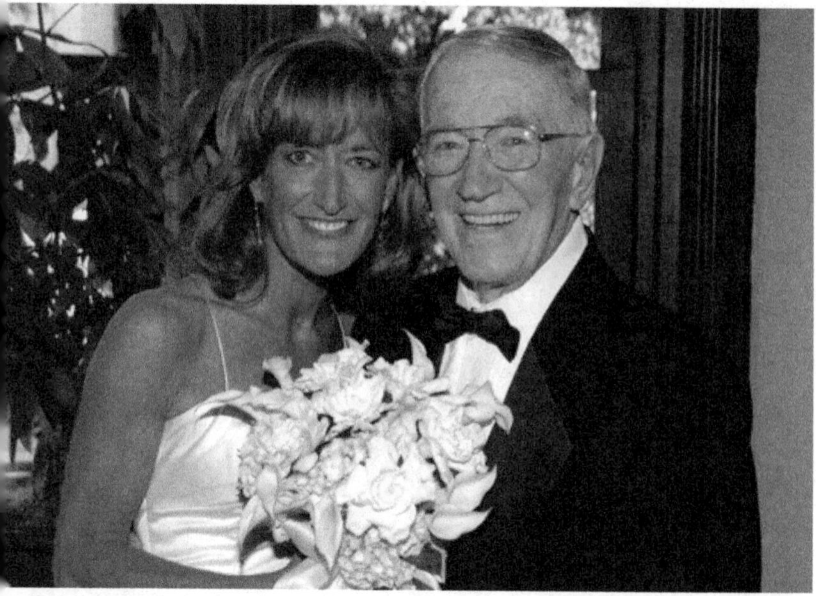

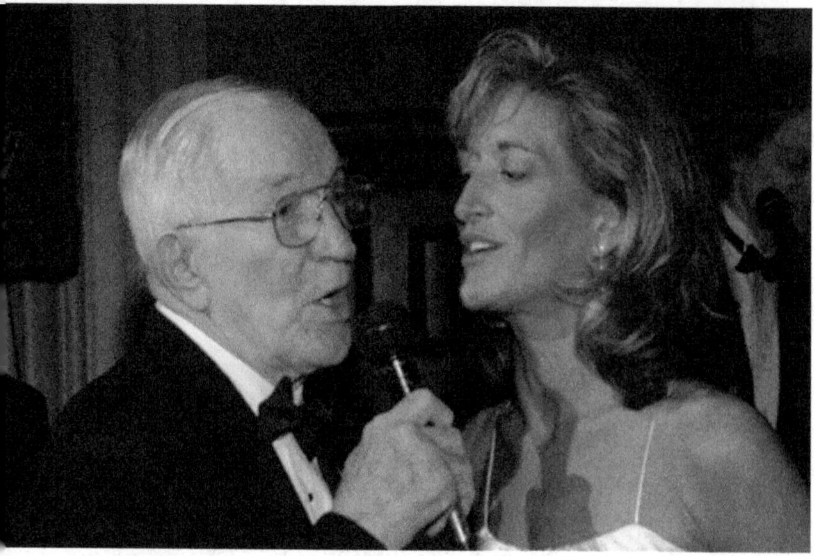

Dad and Laurie at Laurie's Wedding — 2007

*Share some of your insights for working well with others.*

Every day for Breakfast,
You'll be dining with the stars
And for luncheon you'll be munchin
Rainbow candy bars.
You'll be livin' a la Mode
On Jupiter & Mars
"On a Dreamer's Holiday"

(CONT PG 22)

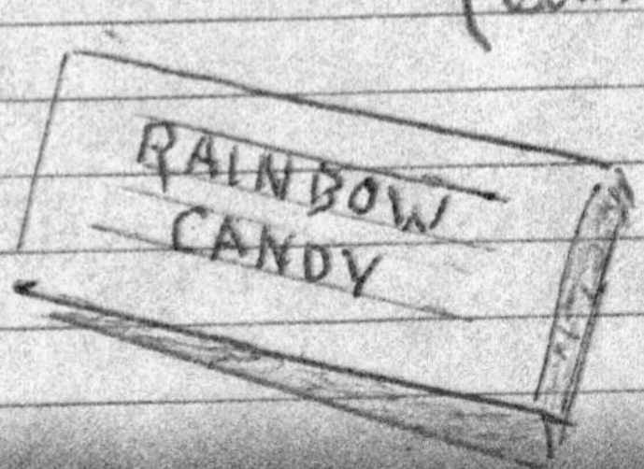
RAINBOW
CANDY

*Did you enjoy reading as a boy?*
*What were some of the most memorable books you read?*

Make it a long Vacation, Time
there is plenty of ~~Lu~~ Ove
You need no invitation.
Just bring along the one you Love.

Help yourself to Happiness,
and sprinkle it with mhrr
Have yourself a dream,
and dream for all your worth

You will feel terrific
when you get back down to earth.

From "A Dreamers Holiday"

END.

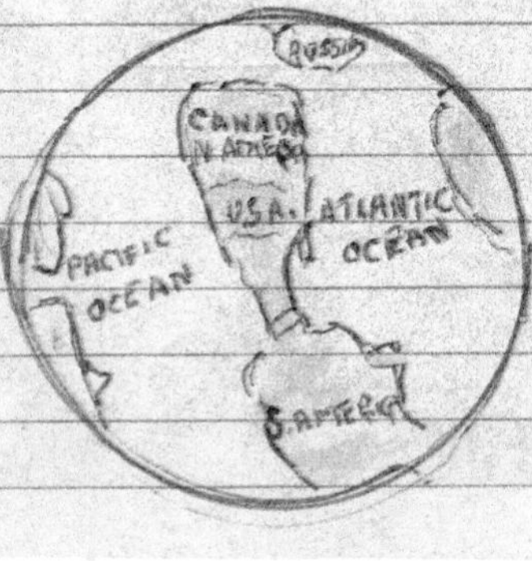
RUSSIA
CANADA
U.S.A.
ATLANTIC OCEAN
PACIFIC OCEAN
S. AMERICA

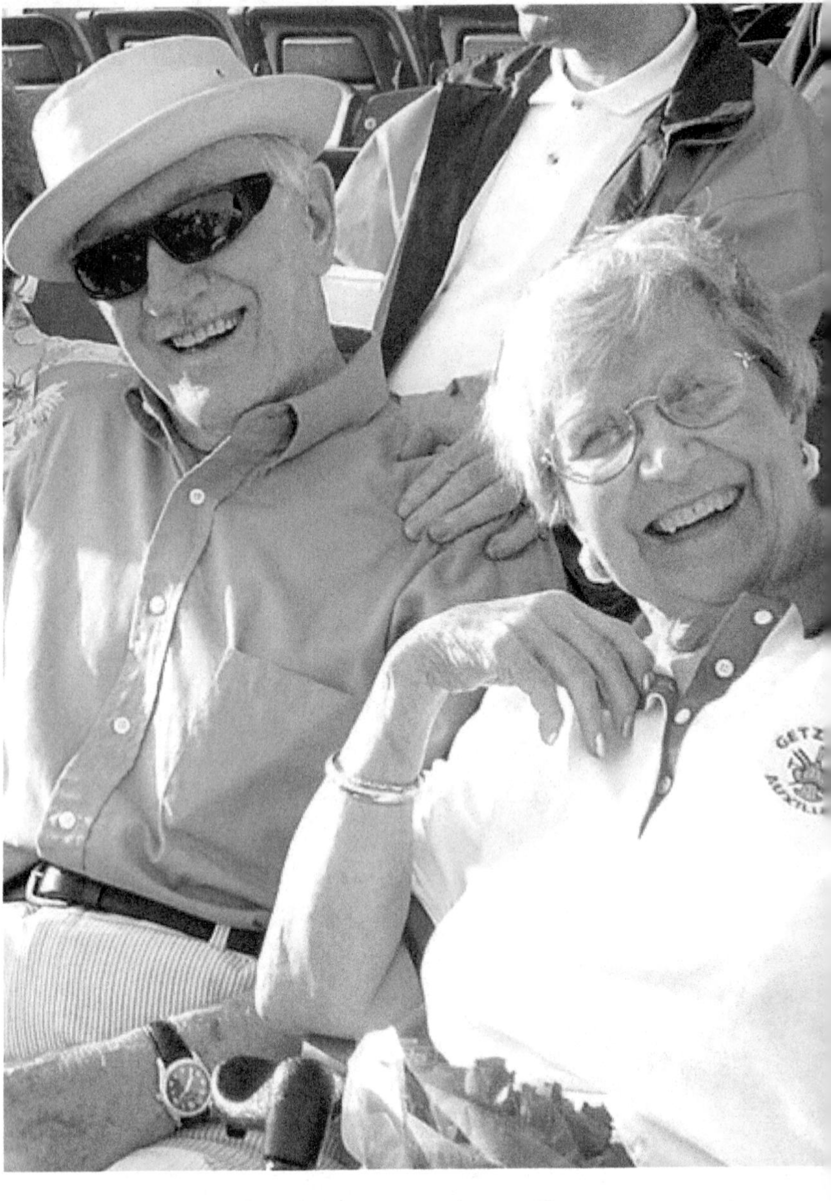

Take Me Out to the Ballgame

Me, my brother Billy, Dad and
my sister Marilyn

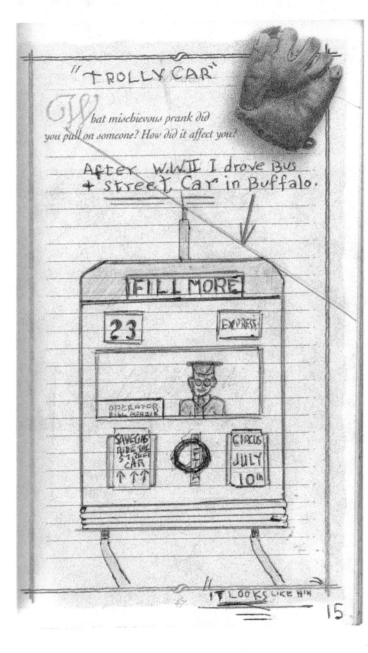

"TROLLY CAR"

*What mischievous prank did you pull on someone? How did it affect you?*

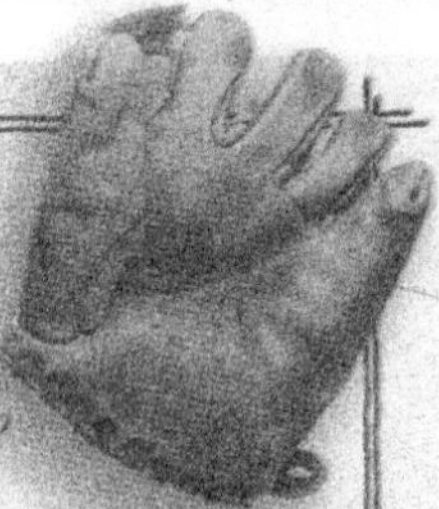

After W.W.II I drove Bus + Street Car in Buffalo.

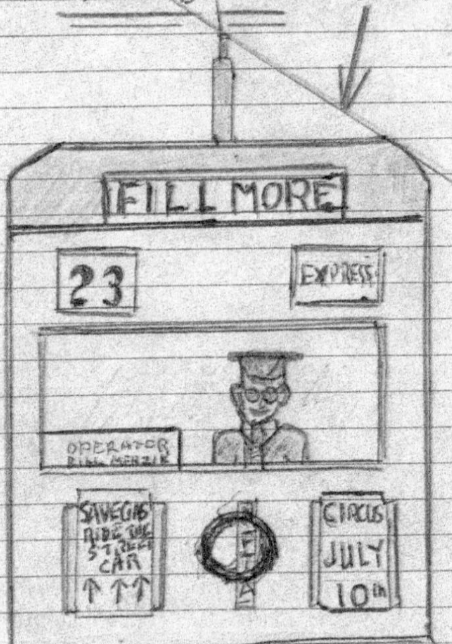
FILLMORE
23
EXPRESS
OPERATOR
SAVE GAS RIDE THE STREET CAR
CIRCUS JULY 10th

"IT LOOKS LIKE HIM"

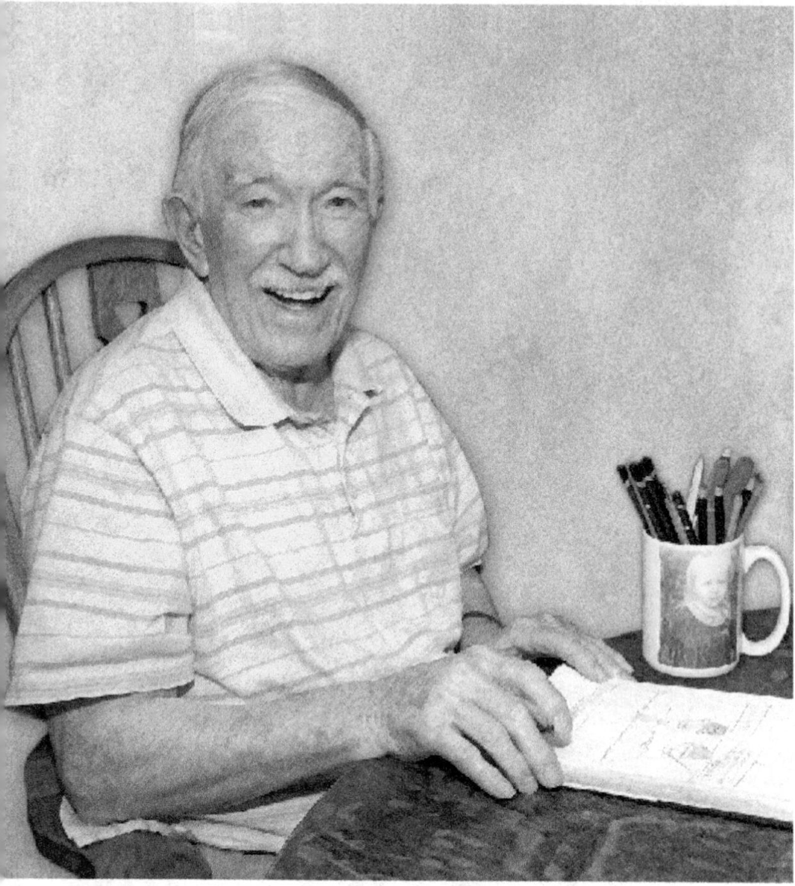

Dad at the Table Drawing Another Cartoon

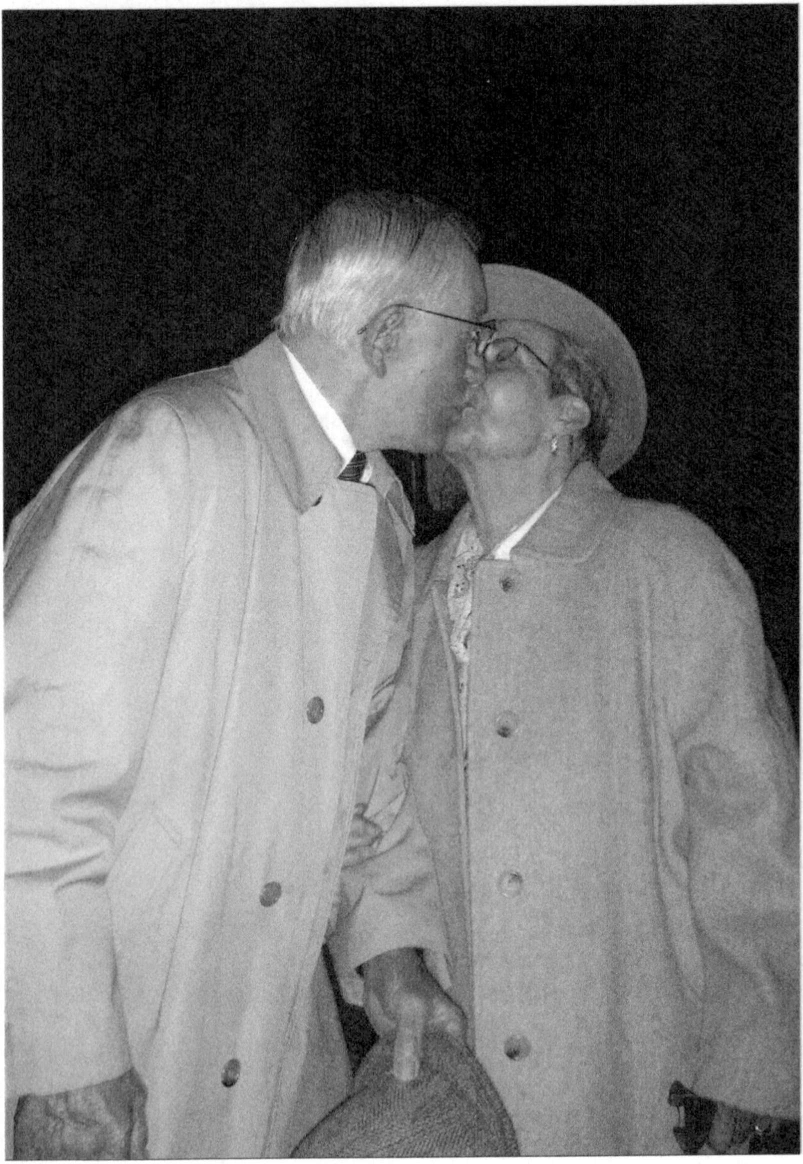

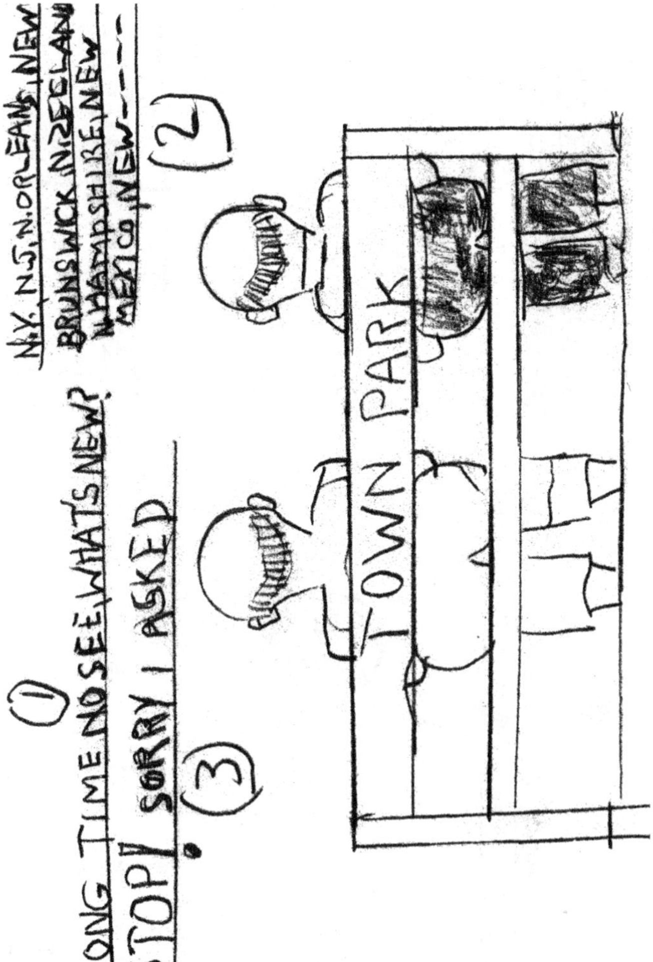

(1)
LONG TIME NO SEE, WHAT'S NEW?
(2)
N.Y., N.J., N. ORLEANS, NEW
BRUNSWICK, N. ZEELAND,
N. HAMPSHIRE, NEW
MEXICO, NEW----
(3)
STOP! SORRY I ASKED
TOWN PARK

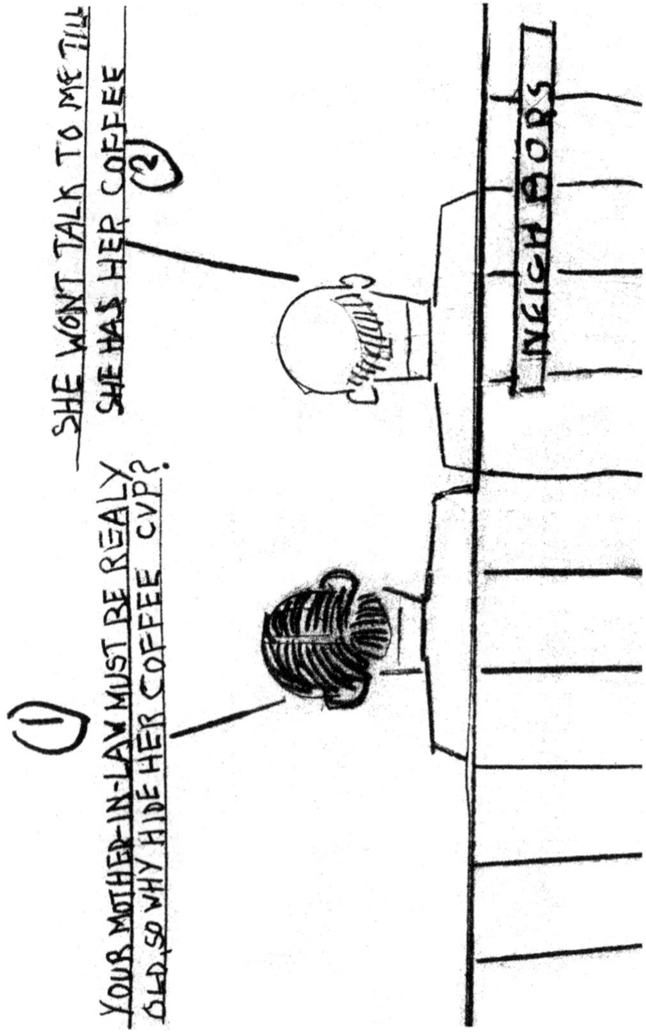

(1)
YOUR MOTHER-IN-LAW MUST BE REALY OLD, SO WHY HIDE HER COFFEE CUP?
(2)
SHE WONT TALK TO ME TILL SHE HAS HER COFFEE
NEIGHBORS

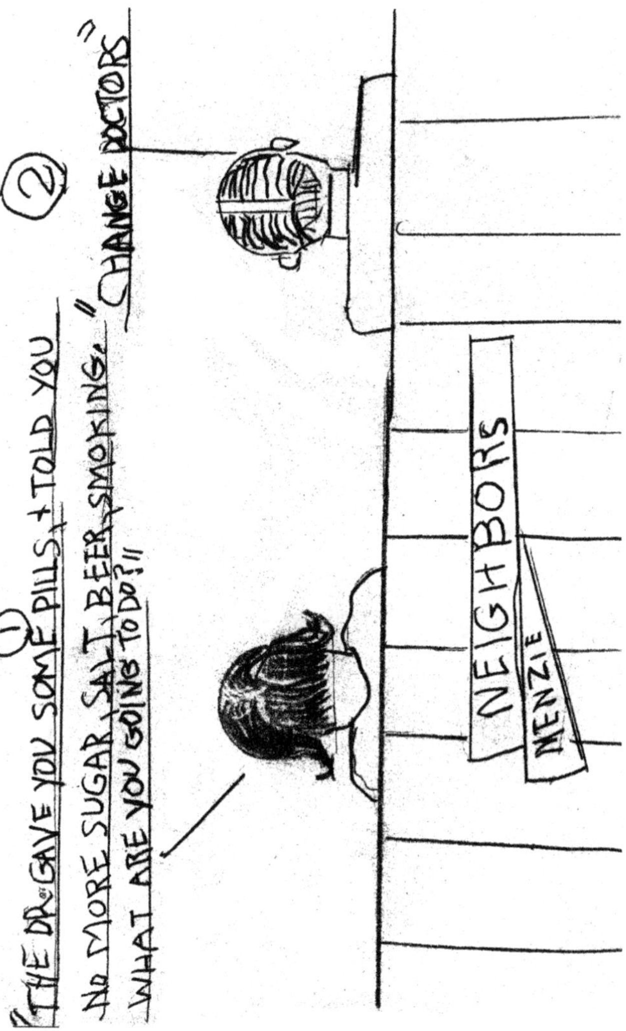

1
"THE DR. GAVE YOU SOME PILLS + TOLD YOU
NO MORE SUGAR, SALT, BEER, SMOKING."
WHAT ARE YOU GOING TO DO?!!
2
"CHANGE DOCTORS"
NEIGHBORS
MENZIE

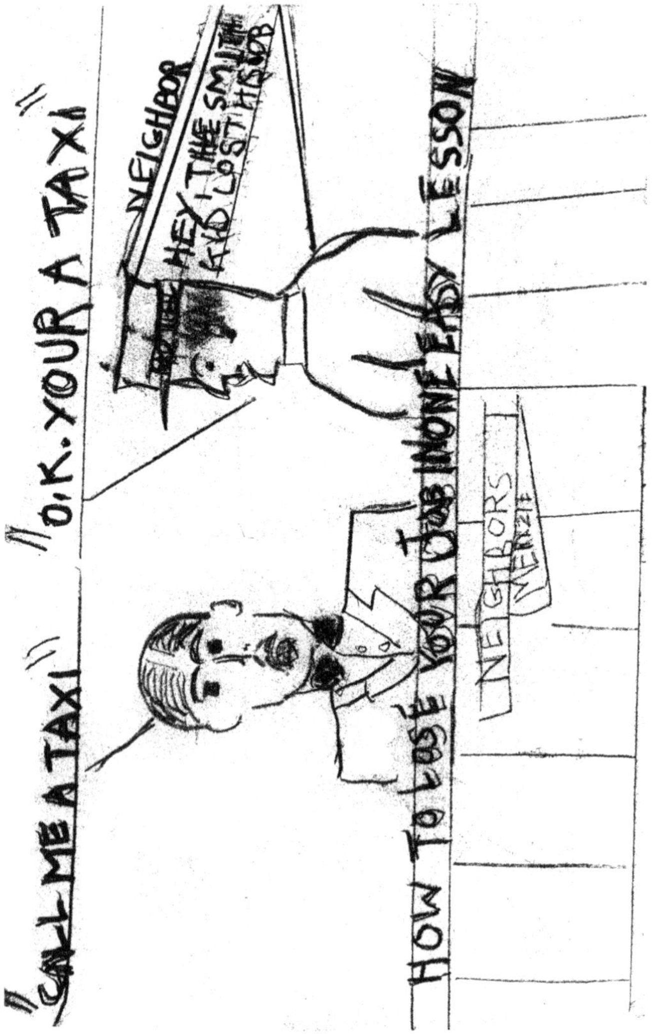
"CALL ME A TAXI"
"O.K. YOUR A TAXI"
NEIGHBOR
HEY, THE SMITH KID LOST HIS JOB
HOW TO LOSE YOUR JOB IN ONE EASY LESSON
NEIGHBORS

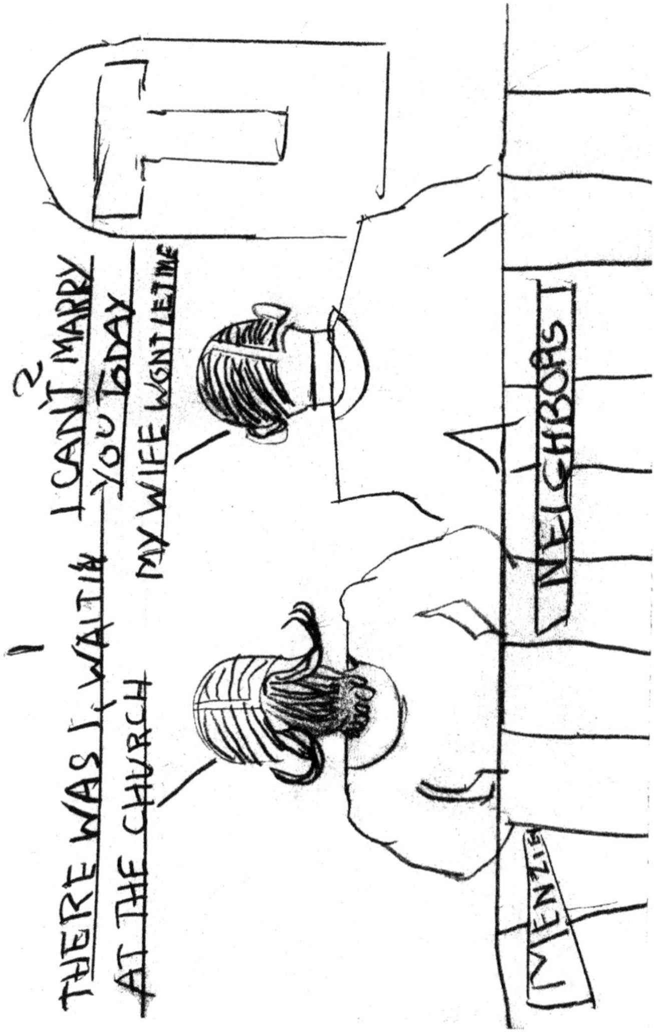
1
THERE WAS I, WAITIN AT THE CHURCH
2
I CAN'T MARRY YOU TODAY MY WIFE WONT LET ME
NEIGHBORS
MENZIES

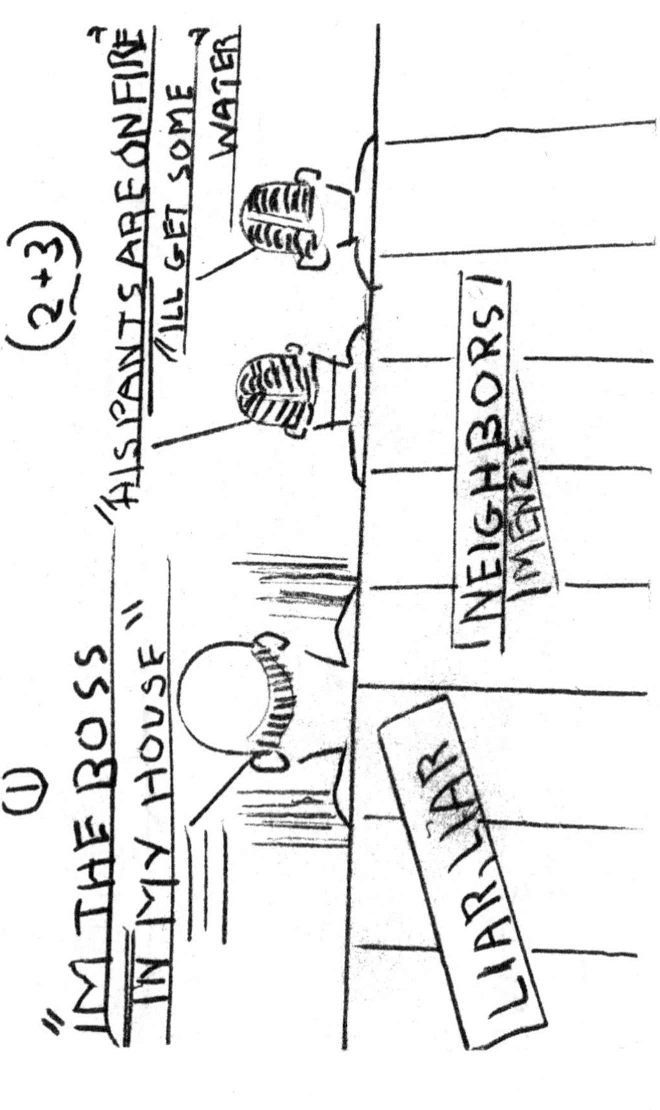
(1)
"I'M THE BOSS
IN MY HOUSE"
(2+3)
"HIS PANTS ARE ON FIRE"
"I'LL GET SOME WATER"
NEIGHBORS!
LIAR LIAR

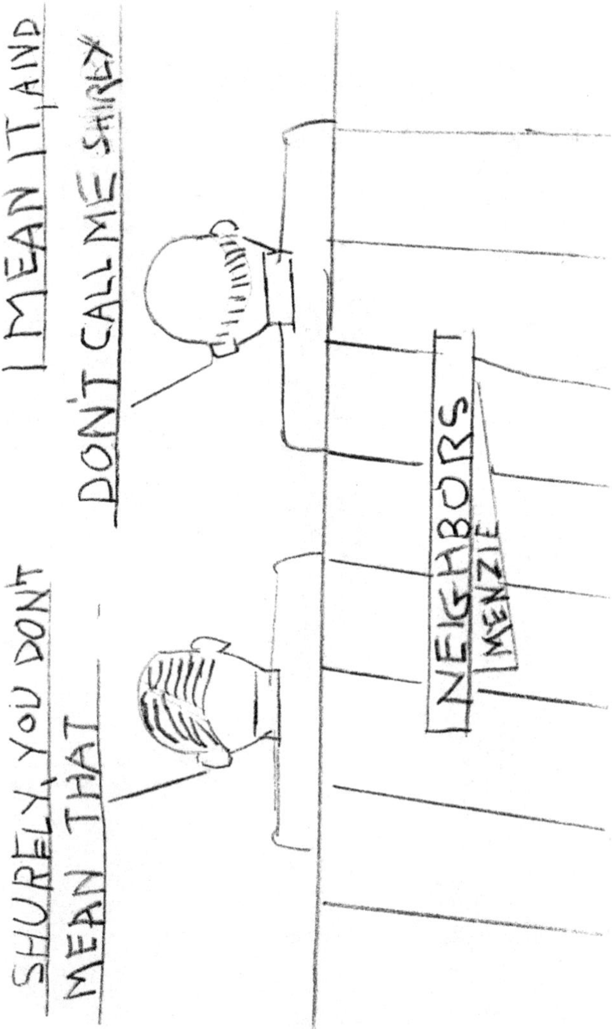
SHURELY, YOU DON'T MEAN THAT
I MEAN IT, AND DON'T CALL ME SHIRLEY
NEIGHBORS
MENZIE

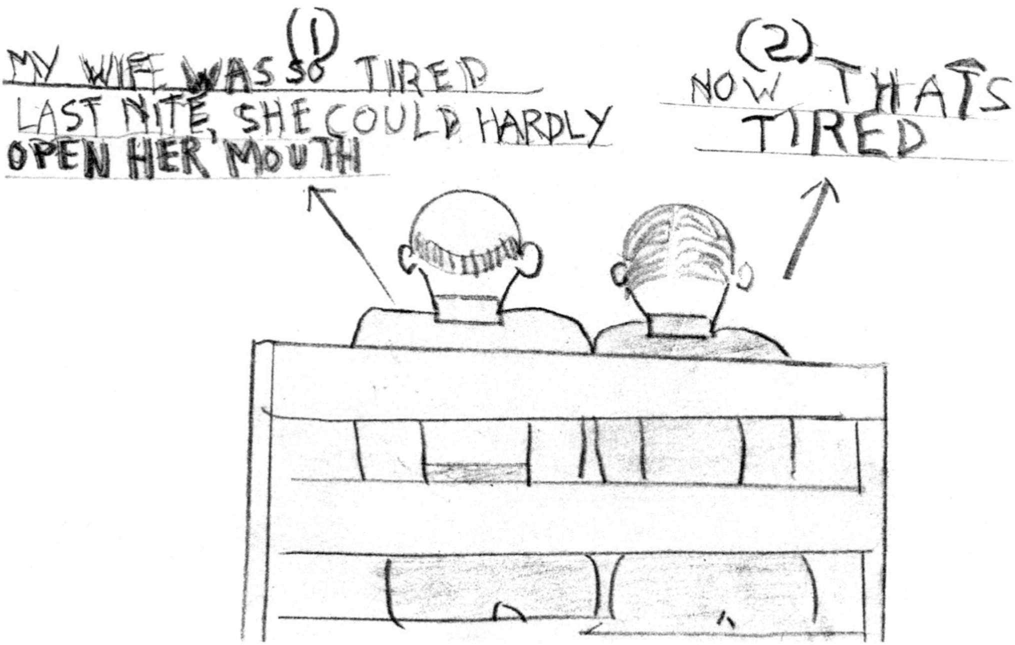
(1)
MY WIFE WAS SO TIRED
LAST NITE, SHE COULD HARDLY
OPEN HER MOUTH
(2)
NOW THATS
TIRED

BE MY LOVE

'CAUSE NO ONE ELSE WILL DO
MY HEART IS CRY

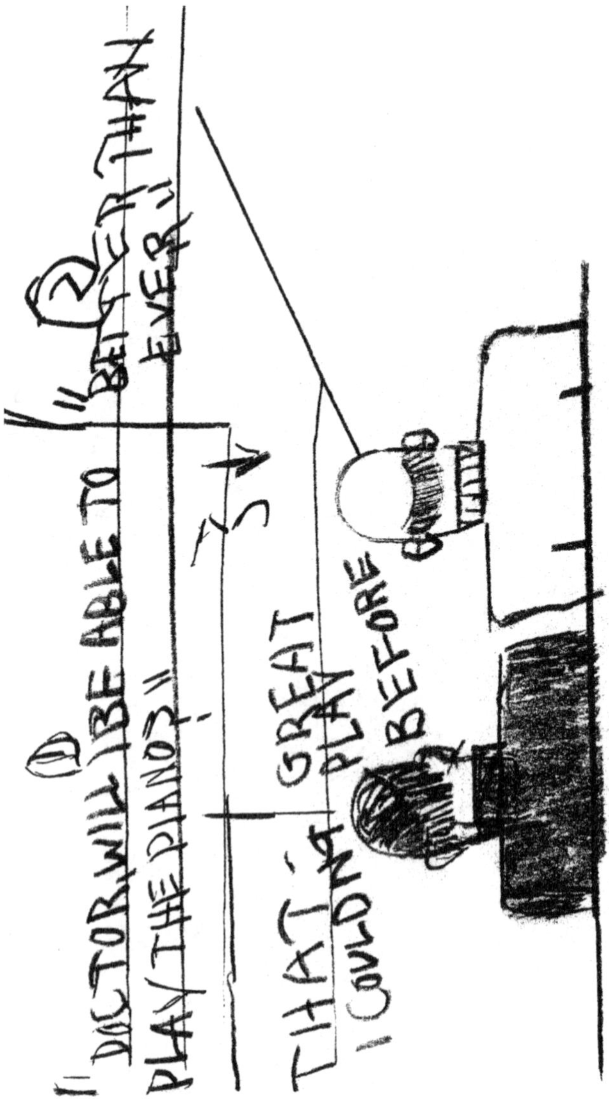
"DOCTOR, WILL I BE ABLE TO PLAY THE PIANO?"
"BETTER THAN EVER"
THAT'S GREAT I COULDN'T PLAY BEFORE

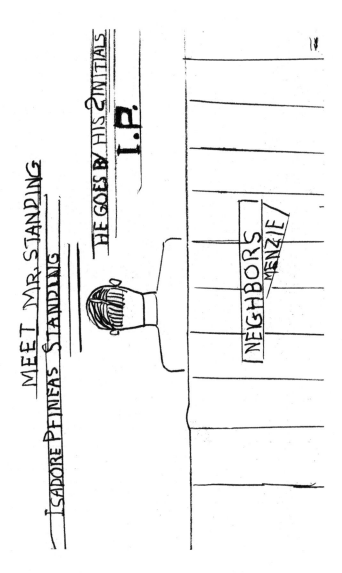

MEET MR. STANDING

ISADORE PHINEAS STANDING

HE GOES BY HIS 2 INITIALS

I.P.

NEIGHBORS

MENZIE!

107

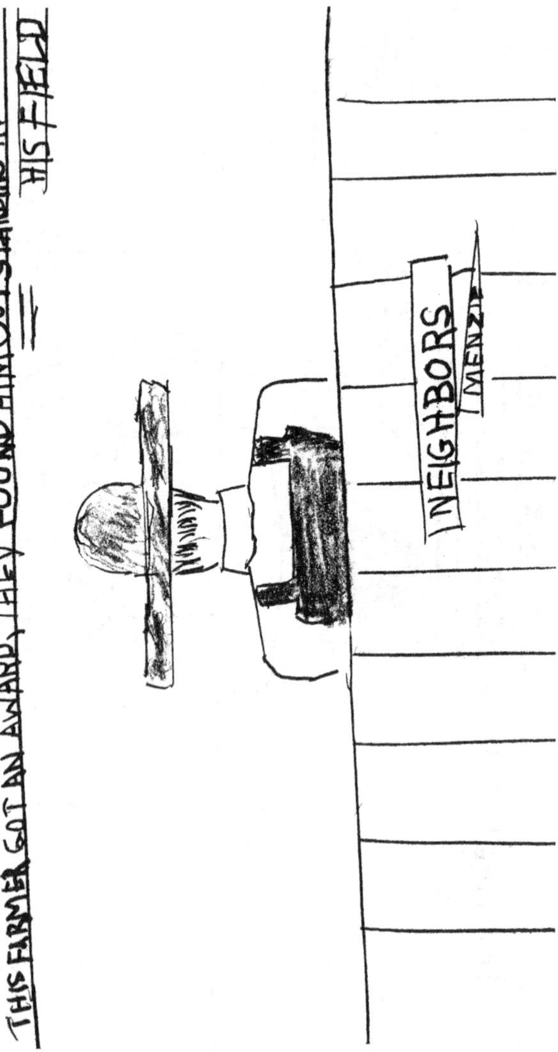
THIS FARMER GOT AN AWARD, THEY FOUND HIM OUTSTANDING IN HIS FIELD
NEIGHBORS

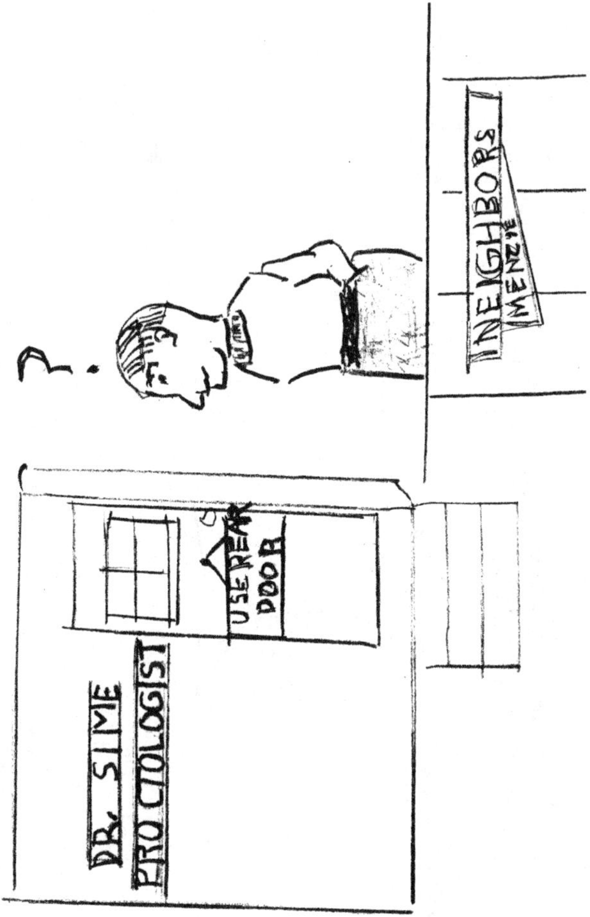
DR. SIME
PROCTOLOGIST
USE REAR DOOR
NEIGHBORS

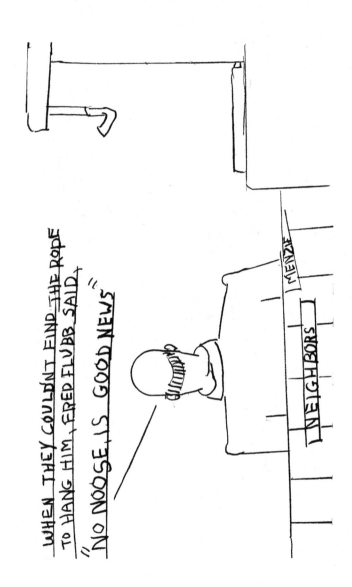

WHEN THEY COULDN'T FIND THE ROPE TO HANG HIM, FRED FLUBB SAID,

"NO NOOSE IS GOOD NEWS"

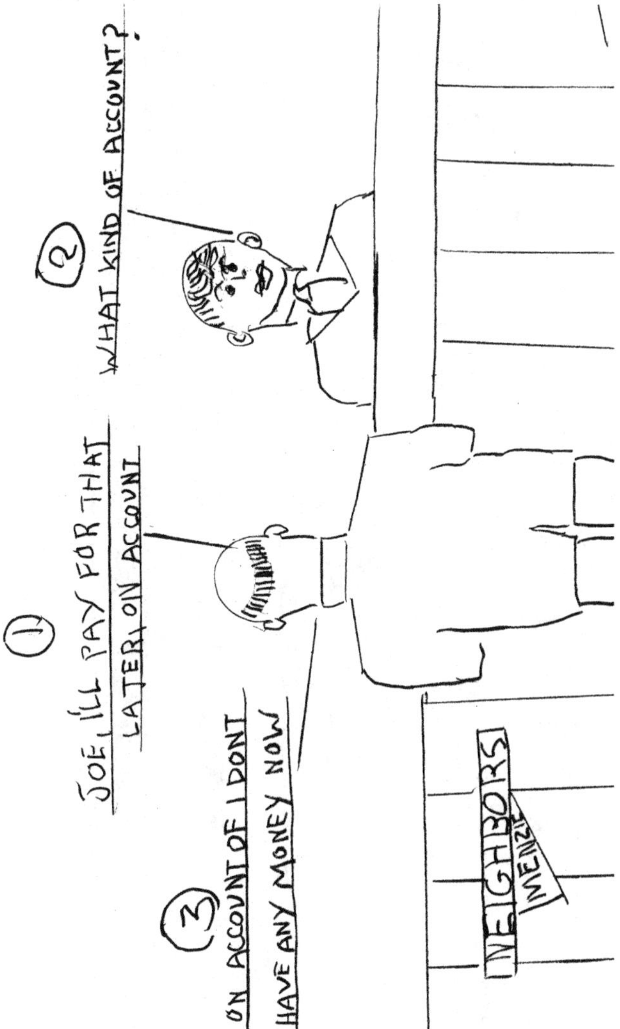
1
JOE, I'LL PAY FOR THAT LATER, ON ACCOUNT
2
WHAT KIND OF ACCOUNT?
3
ON ACCOUNT OF I DONT HAVE ANY MONEY NOW
NEIGHBORS
MENZIE

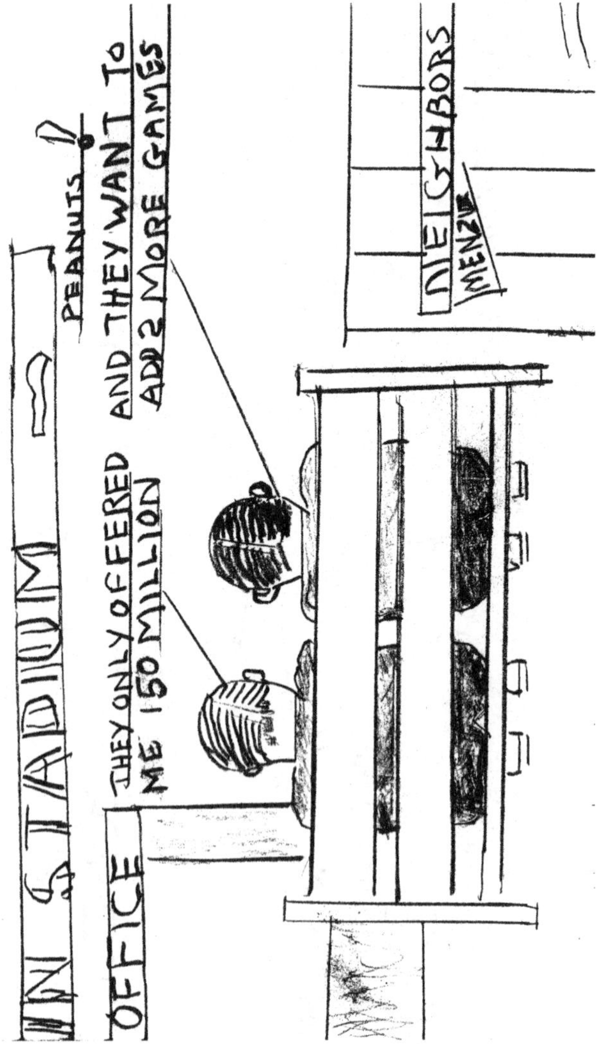
STADIUM
OFFICE
THEY ONLY OFFERED ME 150 MILLION
AND THEY WANT TO ADD 2 MORE GAMES
PEANUTS!
NEIGHBORS
MENZIE

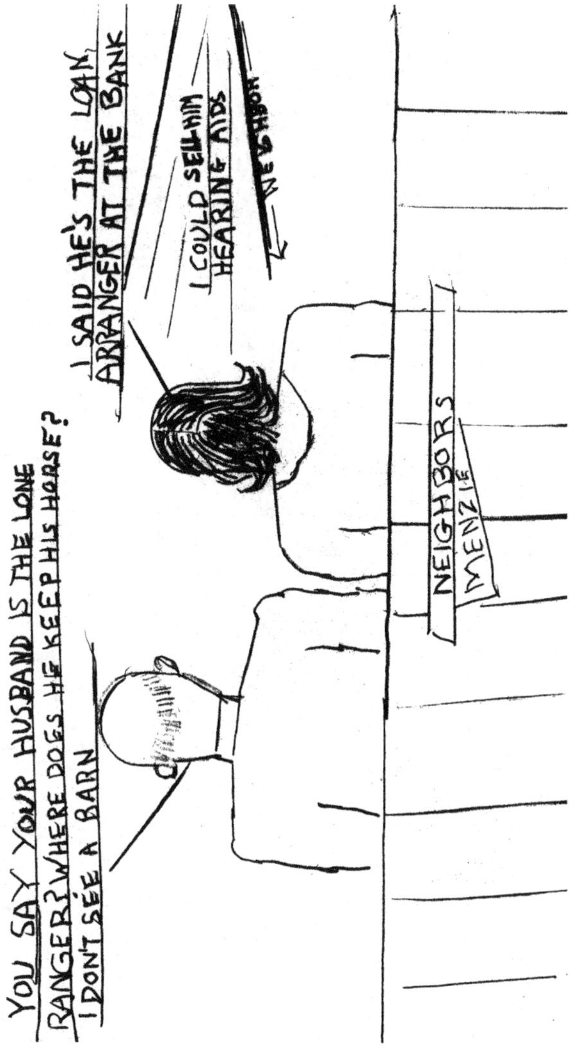
YOU SAY YOUR HUSBAND IS THE LONE RANGER? WHERE DOES HE KEEP HIS HORSE? I DON'T SEE A BARN
I SAID HE'S THE LOAN ARRANGER AT THE BANK
I COULD SELL HIM HEARING AIDS
NEIGHBORS
MENZIE

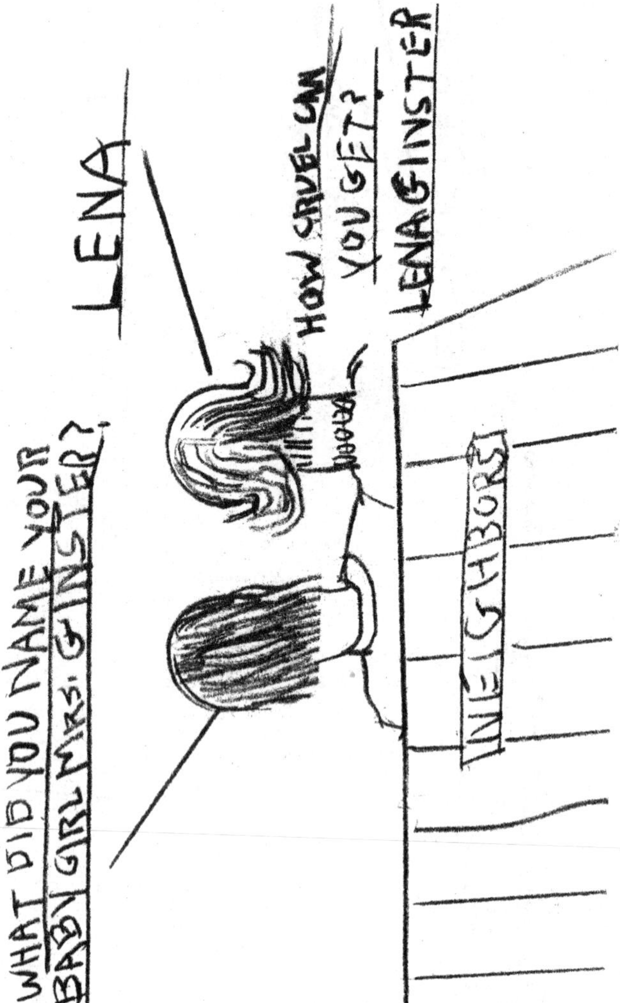
WHAT DID YOU NAME YOUR BABY GIRL MRS. GINSTER?
LENA
HOW CRUEL CAN YOU GET? LENA GINSTER
NEIGHBORS

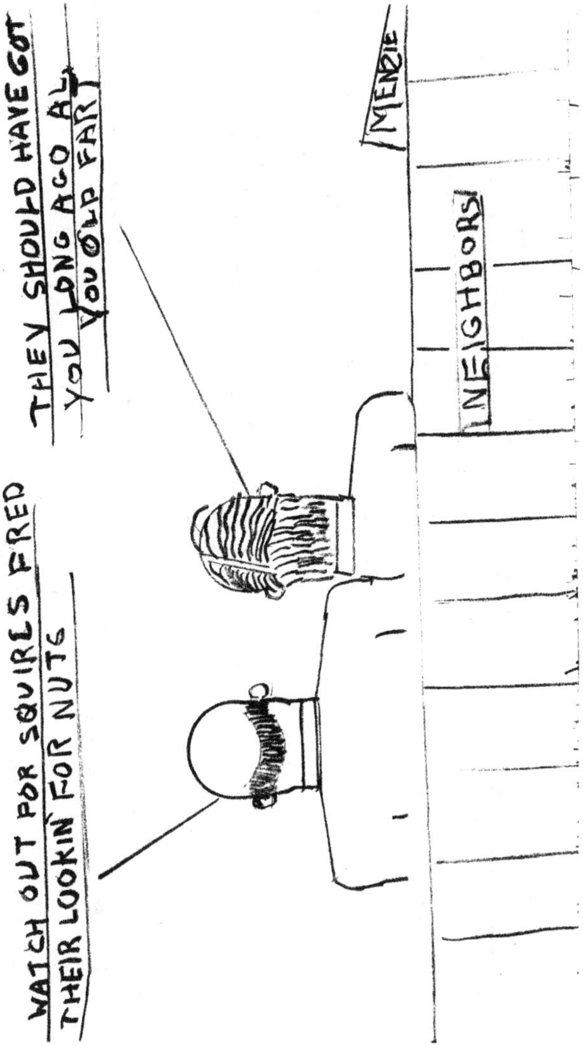
WATCH OUT FOR SQUIRLS FRED
THEIR LOOKIN' FOR NUTS
THEY SHOULD HAVE GOT YOU LONG AGO AL
YOU OLD FART
MENZIE
NEIGHBORS!

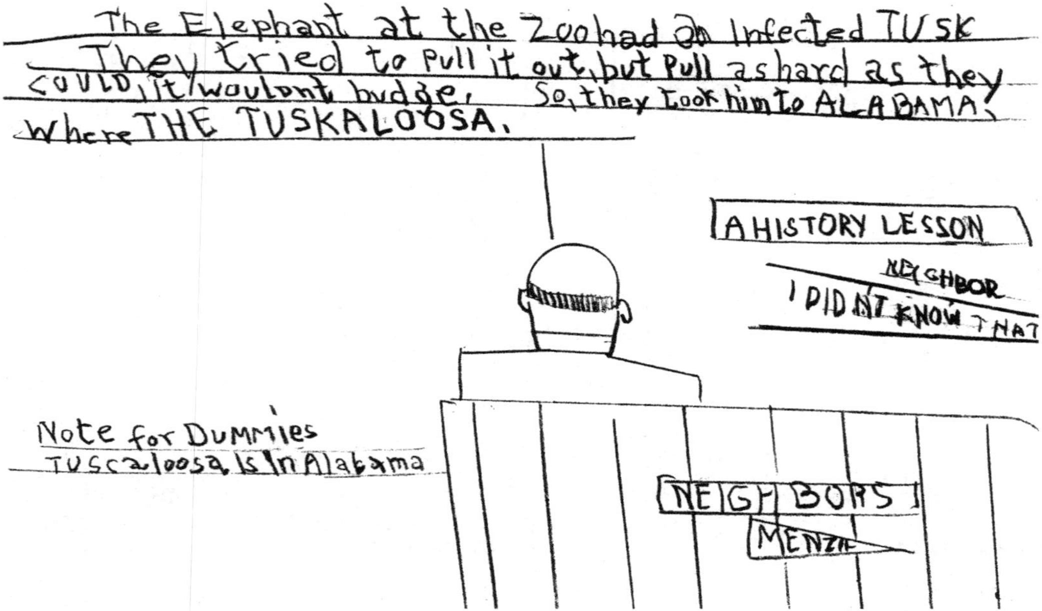
The Elephant at the Zoo had an Infected TUSK
They tried to pull it out, but pull as hard as they could, it woulont budge. So, they took him to ALABAMA, where THE TUSKALOOSA.
A HISTORY LESSON
NEIGHBOR
I DIDNT KNOW THAT
NEIGHBORS
MENZA
Note for Dummies
Tuscaloosa, Is In Alabama

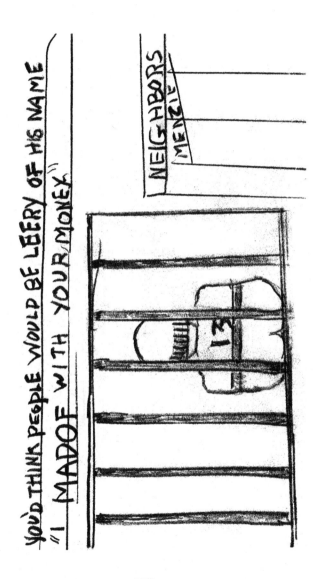

YOU'D THINK PEOPLE WOULD BE LEERY OF HIS NAME

"I MADOF WITH YOUR MONEY"

NEIGHBORS
MENZIE

117

# MENZIE SEZ

I THOUGHT I MADE A MISTAKE ONCE
BUT I WAS WRONG / NEW !!!

A DUCK SEZ GIVE THE BAR A DRINK
THE BARTENDER SEZ "HOW YOU GONNA
PAY?" DUCK SEZ "PUT IT ON MY
BILL"

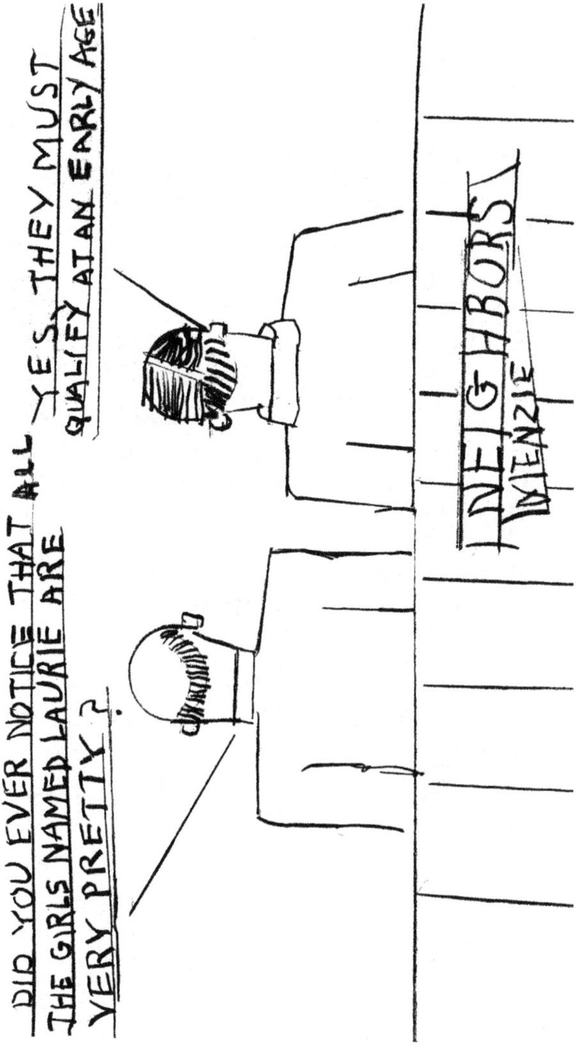

DID YOU EVER NOTICE THAT ALL THE GIRLS NAMED LAURIE ARE VERY PRETTY?
YES, THEY MUST QUALIFY AT AN EARLY AGE
NEIGHBORS

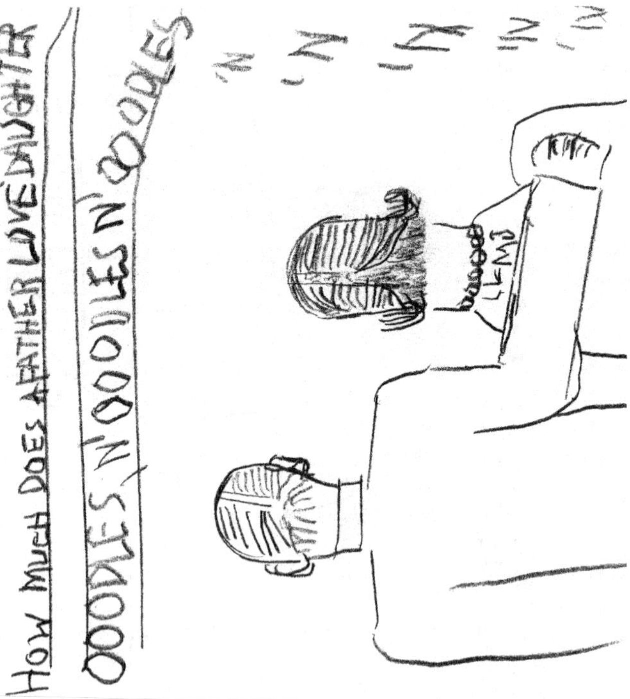
HOW MUCH DOES A FATHER LOVE HIS DAUGHTER
OOODLES N' OOODLES N' OOODLES
Z Z Z Z Z

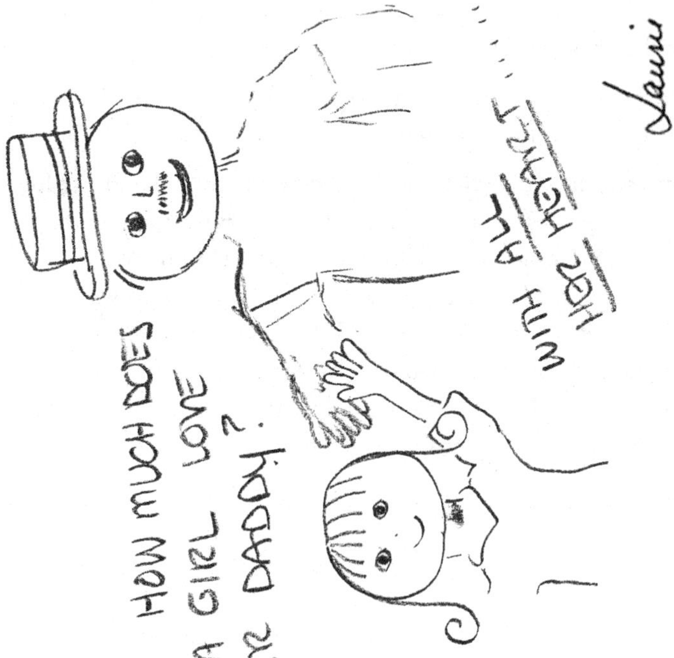
HOW MUCH DOES A GIRL LOVE HER DADDY?
WITH ALL HER HEART......

Daddy created the drawings in this book at the age of 94. At that time, he had lost the ability to walk without assistance and we were told he needed full-time care.

My family was blessed that Dad was able to stay in his home and draw at his own table. It was possible because he and Mom had created a *Plan for Aging*.

As their daughter, I wanted my parents to be happy. As their Elder Law Attorney, I understood the need to have a plan.

Every day, I help older people and their families find and pay for the care they need. In my parents' case, we utilized a program called the **Nursing Home Transition and Diversion Waiver**, offered by New York State Medicaid. This program allows qualifying seniors to remain in their homes while receiving care that would otherwise have to be provided in a nursing home. Because of this plan, Mom and Dad were able to live together through 70 years of marriage before he died.

At *Pfalzgraf, Beinhauer & Menzies, LLP*, we create an individualized *Plan for Aging* for each of our clients.

This *Plan for Aging* coordinates your legal, financial, and health care needs so you or your loved one can age with peace of mind.

We do this by:

- Organizing financial resources to determine a baseline for your plan

- Making sure your legal documents are coordinated to preserve and distribute your assets most effectively

- Working with a Geriatric Care Manager to determine the best plan for your care and safety

- Maximizing the use of public benefits and private resources to reach your goal

If you have questions, concerns, or would like a consultation, please feel free to call us at 716.204.1055.

———————

## Pfalzgraf Beinhauer & Menzies LLP
### Counsel for Generations®

455 Cayuga Road, Suite 600
Buffalo, New York 14225
716.204.1055

(w) PBMLawyers.com
(e) information@PBMLawyers.com

CPSIA information can be obtained
at www.ICGtesting.com
Printed in the USA
FSOW03n0353090217
30534FS

9 780990 649724